HOW SOCIAL RESOURCE INFLUENCES ORGANIZATIONAL

RESOURCE SUPPLY

JOHN LOK

Copyright

2021 MAR. First Print Published

Contents

Preface

Introduction

Any organizations must need resources to be provided in order to supply for their organizational development. However, resouces may include human resources, equipment facilities resources , earth natural resource e.g. land, water wood, gas et. building material resources, even working time resources , technological etc. different kinds of resources. Thus, it seems that any organizations must need some resources to help their organizational daily operation in success.

The question concerns what the best resources used strategies to be achieve the most efficiency or the best performance to be organizational development as well as how and why social resource may influence organizatioal resource supply.

In my these series, I shall explain what factors may influence an organizations to use that resources in the most efficient effectiveness in order to avoid to waste nature or human or material resources . Readers can learn what the strategies may be applied to avoid organizational wasting resource behaviors. In my this book four series, I shall apply how and why organization resource shortage can bring what influence to organizational and social change.

How can business apply right or reasonable science management principle to manage that businesses effectively and efficiently in order to achieve sale and profit raising aim in the least resource suitation? Otherwise, applying wrong or unreasonable science management principle , it can bring what disadvantages or negative impacts to the businesses. IN my this chapter, I shall attempt to indicate above questions . Readers can have more clear view whether why the kinds of science resource management methods are not suitable to be applied to the kind of organizations to bring negative impact consequences.

Prologue

must be the most important factor to influence its sale success. Information technology internet speed, online webstore design, online transation convenience transaction feeling (tangibale and intangible both resource factors) may influence its future clients number ? p.86-105

How an ecommerce organization resource affects ssociety?

Why has online webstore's information technology resource close relationship to influence online buyers number and social job chance?

How do organizational resources affect organizational change?

How to build organizatonal resource using right psychology

How psychological method help employees to avoid resource waste

Chapter 5
OUTSOURCING SERVICE RESOURCE AVOIDS WASTE STRATEGY

●

Information Technology Outsourcing p.106-116
●

Outsourcing or insourcing in human resource
supply chain factor
●

Global outsourcing source strategy
in a value supply chain
●

Outsourcing benefits in economic view
●

What motivate outsourcing and what is being
outsourced risk and concerns?
●

How can choose smarter outsourcing?
●

What is environmental uncertainty factor?
●

Whether outsourcing will bring
what kind of work skills.

● Bibliography
Chapter 6 Robots whether can help organizations to avoid
resource waste

Chapter 7
How social resource influences organizational resource supply

Human Behavioral network job brings social
economic benefits
    What does human network job mean
    Why human network job behavior may influence economy

Robots take our jobs behavioral and economy influences
    Robot job behavior brings economy influences

Intellectual human economic behaviors
What does intellectual human economic behaviors
mean ?
    The relationship between social change and human
behavior

How human productive behavior may influence economic development

- New Zealand farmer individual wine productive behavior
- America high technological productive behavior
- China share market investing behavior

Why has any individual country have many people invest share behavior which can influence the country's macro consumption desire?

Can technology influence human shopping behavioral change?

Why and how human behavior may influence the country's economic growth or recession?

Technology how impacts human behavior changing?

How and why employees behaviors may influence economy development?

Robots invention whether they can help organizations to raise efficiencies or inefficiencies? p.161-190

- New Zealand farmer individual wine productive behavior
- America high technological productive behavior
- China share market investing behavior

CHAPTER ONE

Internet will be intangible technology knowledge resource to organizations

New economy brings new way of resource management. The old loyalty and job security -based organization changes, organizations know that the assets are largely made up employees (HRM), but many new organizations begin to believe technology is important assets, such as Amazon is global ecommerce delivery service organization. It seems internet high technology is its important intangible resource to help it earn global e-buyers number increases . So , many organizations began to believe that technology will be important resource, such as internet can provide online business chance. With all the businesses are taking full advantage of internet, for example, the US department estimates that the value of retail e-commerce in 2000 year was about $25 billion, which represents less than 1% of US retail sales. Despite this, interest in e-business remains high.

● Why internet may be main technology resource to organizations?

E-commere needs strategy in order to win competitors, questions include: What criteria do customers use to choose between our firms and competitors? How do the best employees decision whether to join? What business environment attracts and keeps the best suppliers making with our firms? What characteristics draw the most royal invesdtors to our firms? e.g. Amazon . com's web site and Wal-mart's can apply internet technology resource to create each e-store to let e-buyers to choose any kinds of products to buy athome conveniently. Hence, internet technology, even future other kinds of new technology may be main technology resources to organizations, when they can help organizations to raise sale competitive effort.

I mean that digital economy will be one kind new digital resource to future any organizations. The essential piece is the knowledge, it is what give it life and what makes it an interesting and fulifulling purchase and sale channel for people to spend their time , such as e-commerce virtual organization may be leaded to let purchase and ale transactions carry on easily from online websites. Hence, internet may be main knowledge management (intellectual capital) resource to any e-commerce organizations. It is about the storage, transfer knowledge.

For Amazon publish example, e-books will be knowledge as an object, like a book in library. Amazon can apply internet technology to help it to sell any author's ebooks from its book estores. So, ebooks are Amazon's knowledge resources to help it to create readers incomes. E-books is intangible knowledge resource to Amazon . Any authors' paper and ebooks will be sold cheap price to help Amazon to attract global readers to choose to buy its ebooks from its different countries e-webstores at home conveniently.

Hence, any e-commerce organizations also need HRM (emanagers) to help them to deliver a superior value (world class capabilities) in both te virtual and physical world. E-management will be another main human resources to e-commerce organizations. Why does e-management will be future main HRM resource to e-commerce organization? The reasons may include:

E-management demands in sort of managerial/e-commerce sale strategy effort, skills at positioning the firm within a networm of industries, e-management also demands the ability to see how the firm fits into a value creation-e-management is different because doing it work requires the e-engineering of business eco-systems, e-management demands the ability to be connected to thousands of inputs about specific changes among many industry participants , such as suppliers , customers, employees, competitors, media and shareholders.

Effective e-management requires the ability to monitor developments that can change with unusually high frequency. However, it is also essential that e-managers distinguish between the few meaningful inputs and the many inputs that have limited significance, ability to sustain organizational change, effectie e-managers monitor changes in their markets. So, instead of e-commerce organizations need to employ talent e-managment staffs to help them to manage overall e-commerce organizations. E-leading staffs (HRM) is another main HRM need. E-leaders need to know how to design online brochures, e.g. online brochures simply involved putting a company's market materials on the web. in order to attract or persuade online buyers visit its websites and choose the most right price of product to buy easily. E-leaders need to lead front-office transactions which involved putting customer facing customers , such as placing on order on the web when leaving back-office activities, such as order fulfillment unchanged.

E-leaders also need to integrate online online purchase transactions in which a firm actually linked its front -office and back -office systems and processes in a fashion, e.g. most companies have developed online brochures , in order to let online advertisement tool to attract e-buyer individual purchase choice from its webstores. Hence, future any e-commerce organizations must need (HRM (e-leaders and e-managers) to help them to bring innovation in order to achieve maximize profit aim. So, internet webstores, e-leaders , e-managers may be future e-commerce organization main resources. So, e-commerce organizations, manages are actors at three levels: In the front line , as entrepreneurs, in the middle , as facilitators, and integrators, at the top as institution builders.

Hence, future new economical society, it creates e-commerce organizations number increases, when consumers began to accept online purchase transaction activities. Hence, it causes e-commerce began to feel internet (e-webstores, e-leaders, e-managers), they will be the most influential resources (intangible knowledge managment and tangible URM both resourcees to influence their success or failure.

● Why doe e-commerce organization believe (e-webstore design, e-leaders and e-managers) will be main organizational resources?

The most important question: It asks when e-buyers visit their webstores, wo are their target customers and shich needs of theirs are their trying to satisfy? For exap,e many airlines , e.g. American airlines, China airlines began to feel online e-tickets sale channel is more easily than paper ticket shop sale channel, because many air passengers began to accept e-ticket/ online ticket purchase choice more than visiting airline shops . They feel that they do not want to waste time to visit airline shops. They like to pre-book to buy e-ticket to pay from the airline e-websote conveniently. Hence, e-webstore design knowledge management , e-leaders and e-management webstore management skill will be future any one e-commerce organizations their main tangible and intangible resources (assets) to help their e-commerce businesses development.

On conclusion, I believe that the current economy is not a high-tech economy or an internet economy, not an m-commerce economy , but instead customer econoomy. Customers need to gather with information and access, they are demanding, fair, global price, they are demanding that compares deal with them using the distribution channel , they choose manufacturing direct and through dealers and retailers. Base on those factors, they encourage future many e-commerce organizations cause organization change traditional resouce concept, such as land, capital equipment, tangible resource began to change to e-commerce organization's intangibel and tangible resource, such as knowledge management to e-online web store design skills, e-leaders and e-managers e-stores sale management strategy and e-buyer product research and brochure online advertisement design skill. All of these knowledge management skill will be future organizations' main resources to help them to create new economic competition effort.

CHAPTER TWO

Organization resources defination

What are organizational resources ? What do organizational resources mean? What kinds of organizational resources are needed? What negative impact may be influenced if organizations lack enough resources to influence organizational development? Does working time belong to organizational time resources to influence employee individual efficiency e.g. how arranging enough employee to do the identified task in the most short time in order to achieve the most efficient performane? I shall attempt to identify examples to explain above questions as below:

In general, organizational resources are all assets, that are available to a firm for use during the production process. The four basic types of organizational resources are human, monetary , raw materials and capital. Organizational resources are combined, used and transofrmed to finished products during the production process. For organizational human resource example, human resource activities full under the following five core functions: staffing, development, compensation, safety and health core functions.

● HR resource

HR conducts a wide variety of activities. However, in any organizations, the major resources used by organizations are often described as follow (1) human resources (2) financial respirces (3) physical resources and (4) information resources. Managers are responsible for acquring and managing the resources to accomplosh goals. Hence, in organizational HR aspect, it may include these function, such as retirement and selection, performance management , learning and development, succession planning, compensation and benefits, human resource information systems. Because considering that for many organizations employees themselves represent a significant cost to the business, if the organization can use its employees in efficiency.

Then, it can avoid human resource in excess or in surplus on wasting challenge. Then , its employee cost or salary can be reduced. I t means that it does not need to employ in excess employees number, but the organization can still achieve itself the most efficient performance. Hence, any organizations must need to learn how to avoid " in excess employees number supply or wasting employee working behaviors" challenge . Because if some tasks do not need many employees to work together, it can still be achieved efficiency . Then , the organization ought not employee too many or excess employees to finish the kind of task. Thus, learning how to use efficient human resources, it can help organizations to avoid wasting working time to any departments employees. For example, when one factory has limited land to be supplied to become warehouse in order to help it to keep sticks. If it has excess logistic or factory workers number. Then, they are wasting working time to do not important tasks in warehouse, it means that if the factory has only one warehouse, but its area is small, it can allow maximum 50 workers to stay in the warehouse , but the warehouse has above 100 workers are staying to deliver goods in the small warehouse . Then, they must not actieve the most efficiency , even their delivery or transport goods performance will be influenced to worse by noise and crowd warehouse working environment. Hence, excess employees number in any working environment, which can not improve organizational performance or riase efficiency any organizations can not neglect " excess employees number" organizatinal HR resource arranging issue.

The solution concerns arranging the most right or the most exact empllyees number in order to supply to any organizational departments. Then, the organization can avoid wasting employee individual talent, reducing employing cost, improvig performance, achieving the most efficiency. Resource capacity means resource pool who are available in the organization to take up to appropriate human resource arrangement to assist any departmental development in long term efficiency. Hence, organizational human rsources may become talent tangible assets or foolish tangible assets. It depends on how the organization's resource capacity tasks arrangement to every employee in different departments. If the organization neglects how to arrange every employee task in the most exact or the most appropriate employees number in the department.

The department's efficiency must be caused worse, because excess employees number, it can not help it to achieve the most efficiency aim, even it may influence the excess employees , themselves feel waste working hours to do the not essential or not important tasks. Then, the organization may cause talent employee to become foolish employee. Otherwise, the organization's efficiency to be worse, because when the department has not enough employees to work. Then , any one employee may feel hard to work, his/her emotion may be influenced to negative, then his/her workig behavior may b inefficiency or lazy working. On consequence, the organization may bring economic loss, due to employee individual lasy working behavior, negative working emotion, even high working pressure may be caused, when one employee needs to do more , then the employee's task, but his/her salary can not increase. He/she will feel unfair to compare the another department employee, he /she does not need to spend long working hours or overtime to work per day. SO, any organization needs to avoid shortage employee supply or excess employee supply issue to any departments. Appropriare employees number is the best strategy in order to raise overall organizational efficiency.

● Time resource

Instead of human resource, land, raw material, earth natural resource, electricity, gas may be organization resources . Whether time may be organizational resources, organizational time management vires time as a scarce resource that must be invested as effectivity. Time is an infinite resource . If not properly managed on in an organization. It can have a negative impact on both employer's and employee's productivity. So, organizations should ensure that workers are well equipped to manage time in their duties.So, in management view, any organization managers must need to consider how to manage time, eg . how to arrange employees to work in different departments in order to achieve the most efficiency. They need to understand which resources are in short supply and focus on the prioritizing work across shared resources, they need agree on a common approach, they also need to realize resource management is an ongoing process. Thus, time is an often ignored but invaluable resource in any organization. All activities be it procurement.

An organization's time, in contrast, goes largely unmanaged. Although, phone calls, email, instant messages , meetings, they are general daily tasks to any organizations managers, but mangers need to know how to arrange the most urgent tasks in prior. For example, if the manager can not arrange a meeting to the discuss client tomorroe, as well as the manager needs to spend two hours to meeting with overall 200 employees to discuss how to solve improving efficiency challenge tomorroe. So, this manager needs to make choice whether he ought spend two hours meeting to the business client, or two hours meeting to 200 employees. If he chooses to meet the business client tomorrow, he will help his firm to win the important business chance, but he can not discuss how to improve efficiency in order to find the best method to let 200 employees to know tomorrow. Thus, tomorrow time management will be one importat time resource to the manager. The manager needs to arrange tomorrow two hours time how to plan business meting or efficiency imporvement meerting either to his 200 employees or the one business client. Because if the manager decided to meet the client, he must need to spend today time to aplan or organize how to arrange either business proposal content for the business client or organizational operational challenge questions and solutions for his 200 employees . So, today time management is also important time resource to influence tomorrow either the success business meeting or the organizational 200 employees meeting. So, it seems that time management may be one important resource to any managers more than general employees in any organizations.

If the manager can know how to manager his/her time to do any prior tasks, then he/she may help the organization to raise efficiency or improve performance. Otherwise, if the manager can not know how arrange what prior urgent task needs to be finished. Then, worse performance or inefficiency may be influenced to cause. So, if the organization manager can know how to make time arrangement, I believe that he can help the organization employees to raise efficiency more easily.

CHAPTER THREE

Organizational efficient using resources economic method

In behavioral economic view , any organizations can attempt to apply behavioral economy method to use resources efficiently. Organizational excellence framework performance measurement takes a systematic approach . One of the most effective ways of using resources and minimizing that use of work. Calculating task cost in the most efficient economic method to help organizations to reduce cost and avoid resources waste, e.g. using resource management software, technology, planning and taking a systematic approach , which aims to manage the most efficient steps to follow to finish or implement each task in the most shor time as well as avoiding excess employees number.

Organizational resource efficiency means using the organization's limited resources in a sustainable manner when minimising impacts on the organization performance. It allows the organization to create more with less and to deliver greater value with less money. HR, raw matcrial, technology input to carry on any organizational resources efficiently ? Management is the process of using organizational resources to achieve organizational goals of using organizational resources to achieve organizational goals effectively and efficiently through planning , organizing , leading and controlling. An efficient organization makes the most productive use of its resource in the most short time and the most eficiency and the least cost aspects.

● What is efficient use of resources to any organizations in economics?

Economic efficiency implies an economic state in which every resource is optimially allocated to serve each individual or entity in the best way when minimizing waste and inefficiency. whan an economy is economically efficient, any changes made to assist one entity would harm another .

Hence, budget how much spending on resources, e.g. employee saley, office and/or plant technological equipment facilities , before making resource expenditure spending decision. Budget is essnetial to help the organization to deduce resource using and excess purchase waste since budget and resource of organizations have interlock or interconnet relationship. If the organization can make exact udget, then it can avoid excess expenditure or waste resource to use. So, organizations need to acquire a talented resource pool , that can lead projects to success, when any kinds of resources are achieved to be supplied to use inn enough . For example, using an effective enterprise resource management system that delivers capabilities. Regardless of the approach and tools used, organizations must determine how to balance to use any kinds of resources efficiently. Thus, in organizational efficient resource using behavioral economy view, the organizational efficiency factor means that influences the efficiency of the organization's use if its resources can be both internal and external, e.g. how implementing strategic plans, they may include selecting what methods and resources to use, and leadning employees on guideline, working in coalitions with organizations around to deliver those needs in the most resource efficient way.

In organizational studies, resource managemetn is the efficient and one resource management technique of resource leveling, of finding the answers to the question, how to use available resource efficiently, effectively and economically ot organization resource expense. SO , resource management is the process of allocating resources and allocating.

● What is meant by economic using of resource to organizations?

Economic resources are the factors used in producing goods or providing services. Economic resources can be divied into human resources, such as labors and management, and non humann resource, such as land, capital , goods, finished resources and technology , for example, natural resource is a key input in the production process that stimulates economic growth. Natural resources have limited direct economic use in satisfying human need, but transforming them into goods and services enhances their economic value to the socirty. So, if the country has many organizations know how to use their natural resources input in that production processes. Then, they can create themselves economic benefits directly and attribute economic benefit to society indirectly.

Thus, the types of economic organizations can be identified, there are subsistence recipreocal exchange with subsistence, peasant with primary reliance on self-produced food, but containing some exhange elements, market-commercial , redistribution or state socialist. Thus organizations need to learn hoe to use themselves organizational resources efficiently. Organizational resources are all assets that are to a firm for use during the production process. The four basic types of organizational resources are human, monetary, raw material and capital. Organizational resources are combined , used and transformed into finished products during the production process. So, a business that understands how to use resources efficiently. resource management is the process of allocating resources in order for a company to grow easily.

Organizational economic is used to study transactions within individual firms and determine management approach to managing resources. It is broken down into thee major subjects: agency theory, transaction cost economic and property rights theory. Agency theory is a priinciple that is used to explain and resolve issues in the relationship between business principles and their agents. Most commonly, that relationship is the one between shareholders as principles, and company executives as agents. Agency theory is used to understand the relationship between agents and principals. The agent represents the principal in a particular business transaction and is expected to represent the best interests of the principal without regard for seld interest. So, when the relationship between shreholders and company executives is kept the best.

Transaction cost economic is understood as alternative modes of organizing transactions (governance structure, such as markets, firms and bureaus) that mininize transactions costs. This, cost is the primary determinant of such as firm's decision whether it is the most right (the best) or the worst decision. It will influence the firm ho to spend resource behavior. The cost other than the money price that are incurred in trading good and service. SO, if the organization can often make the best decision to carry on any activites. It will avoid to waste resources efficiently. For example, if transaction cost influces the commission, paid to a stockbroker for completing a share deal and booking fee charges when purchase concert tickets. The cost of travel and time to complete an exhange , it means that transaction cost. So if the organization can make the best or the most reasonable decision to carry on any business activities. Then, its transaction cost can be influenced to reduce the most level in order to bring resources economic benefit. e.g. sunk costs are indpeendent of any event and should not resulting from economic trade in a market.

Property right theory means contracted choice, through ownership, property rights theour clarifies the firm's boundary choice. The maon egal property rights are the right of possession, the righ tof excession. So, for the efficiency of property rights al scarce resources are owned by someone. IN the right property rights approsed to the theory of the firm, I assume that in the case of sale ownership by party-property rights define the theoretical and legal ownership of resources and how resources can be used by organizatin. So, above three major organizational theories can assist organizations to know how to spend resources efficiently.

CHAPTER FOUR

The relationship between resource shortage and consumer behavior

Can resource shortage influence consumer behavior changes?

Can bring either positive or negative or both impact to change consumer behavior when the consumer begins to feel resource shrtage occurrence to choose to buy the kind of product or consume the kind of service?

Consumer researchers have suggedsted that chronic resource scaraity, specially, an inproveished early home environment with fewer resources and high levels of instability and uncertainty can lead to chronic differences in choice behavior (Griskevicius et al. 2011). How are consumers affected by scarcity? Scarcity affects producers because they have to make a choice on how to best ise their limited resources. It also affects consumers because they have to make a choice on what services or goods to chooce. Hence, resource shortage may be situational factor influence, situational influences are external circumstances or conditions existing when a consumer makes a purchase decision. Because the kind of product is facing resource shortage issue to influence the product manufacturer can not have enough resource to manufacture the kind og product. SO, number supply is decreasing, such as cars product, if steel number supply is decreasing, it can influence global car manufacture number decreases. When global new car buyers feel that they can not buy any kinds fo new cars easily. Then, even global new car price rises, they won't influence new car buyers purchase desires. So, in new car sale market, if steel supply number reduces, global new car buyer number will not decrease easily.

How does a consumer make choice with scarce resources?

Like producers, consumers also have to make choices, since consumer resources , such as time, attention, and money are limited. They must choose how to best allocate them by making tradeoff. The concept of trade-offs due to scarcity is formalized by concept of opportunity cost. In fact, research in marketing often begins with two assumptions, by scarcity of products and/or a scarcity of resources, dfferent types of scarcity individually and jointly influence.

Consumer behavior , an integrative analysis of research finding remains that scarcity principle in consumer behavior, it refers that scarcity to the condition of resources shortages, it can affect consumer behavior. So, consumer behavior and resource shortage, they seem have close cause and effect relationship between them. For buying behavior example, when one male consumer with high shopping motivations, when he knows a scarcity arrtibute and thus are a vary limited resources, e.g. he allows to buy the product within 5 minutes , when the shop will close soon and thus a very shop time clising time limited. It can persuade the male customer to make purchase decisin immediately. So, it seems that intangible resource , such as shop closing limited time, scarcity may also be a fundamental phenomenon that influences consumer behavior, when the consumer feels that shop will close, it does not allow himw to continue to stay long time in the shop. The shop closing time nay persuade the customer to buy the product immediately.

It explains that why the influence of quantity scarcity and time restriction on consumer, this implies that when consumers' cognitive resources are not restricted by external environmental factor influence, such as shop soon closing time or web traffic to media, when the online buyer , he dislikes to spend long time to click on any website stores to choose themselves brands of the kind of product choice to make purchase decision. The online buyer may only click one website store to make purchase decision immediately.

So, it explains why online sellers can sell their products firm online stores easily, because their website stores web traffic is not busy at the moment. There are not many online buyers click themselves webiste stores at the moment. So, when there are many online buyers can click themselves webstores to choose any kinds of products in shor ttime rapidly. Then, their online sale chance may be influenced by " not busy website stores web traffic jam to media time factor".

Hence, it seems that when one consumer feels resource shortage, it may persuade the consumer to choose to buy the kind of product immediately.

I suggest that people may not only differ in terms of how they choose to consume, this could include encouraging consumers , such as impact pf resource scarcity on price-quality judgement. It means that the predictable " panic shopping" in response, experiencing resource scarcity can also increase a sense of community by encouraging consumer to share shopping experience. So, product uncertainity , which is able to motivate behaviors, such as urgency to buy.

This, scarcity , also is known as paucity, is an eonomics term used to refer to a gap between the buyer purchase desire and external environmental factor, for exmaple time and money are characteristically scarce resources, to urge consumers to make purchases or else they won't guarantee next day purchase the product.

Howveer, the cost of using a resource is called the opportunity cost, the value of the next scarcity in economics connotes not that something is nearly impossible to finf. In common, consumers must choose between correct consumption and future consumption, for example, the COVID 19 crisisi may bring positive urgent time to save product, e.g. medical mouth cover protection product, when many medical mouth cover protection product buyers believe the brand of covid 19 medical moth cover protection products supply is shortage, they believe they ought buy the brand of medical mouth cover protection product supply is shortage, they believe thay ought buy the brand of medical mouth cover protection products immediately.

Otherwise, they can not find this kind of covid 19 medical mouth cover protection products to buy later. So, the anticipation to the covid 19 crisis will help some brands of medical mouth cover protection proucts, they can be sold rapidly . So, panic buying may be encouraged when the covid19 mouth cover protection product buyers feel a common brand share covid 19 mouth cover protection products shortage resource through a collection action. Hence, even the brand of covid 19 medical mouth cover protection products prices are raised, the covid 19 mouth cover buyers still choose to buy the brand of covid 19 mouth cover protection products, because they believe that they can not buy the brand of covid 19 medical mouth protection cover products later, when this brand of covid 19 medical mouth cover manufacturers won't continue to manufacture this kind of covid 19 medical mouth cover products again.

So, it explains that crisis and product sale time limited intangible resources can influence consumers to make a lot purchase decision suddenly. On conclusion, resource scarcity is essentially about current brand for a resource exceeding available supply. Resource scarcity occurs when demand for a natural resource is greater than the available supply leading to a decline in the stock of available resources.

However, limited time may be one kind of intangible resource shortage to influence consumers to choose to make the purchase decision to avoid that they lose the final purchase chance. So, the intangible limited time psychological factor may help businessmen to sell their products in short time, when the consumers feel that they have no enough time to choose any kinds of product to buy or they believe that they can not buy the kind of product later. So, resource shortage may bring position impact to influence consumer behavior in behavioral economy view.

Do they have relationship between organizational resource economic behavior and social needs?

In organizational behavioral economy view, economic systems that shape behaviors and constrain access to resource necessary to organizations and society both. People are influenced to organizations as employees, consumers. IN behavioral economy view, economics is the social science that examines how individuals, businesses and overall societies manage scarce resources. Because none resource exist in unlimited quantities, even internet technology resource , societies must establish priorities and decide how best to allocate resources in such a way that meets as many needs and wants as possible . So, organizational behavioral and economics to explain why employees sometimes make irrational business decisions , and why and how the organization employee individual behavior does not follow the predictions of economic models . Because any organizational employees are emotional and easily distracted brings , they make decisions that are not in their self interest when they are working in organization. Hence, how whether it is more or less any organizations use themselves resource. It may influence the social whether it has much or less resources to society. It can use which interact within the organization,

Why have they interaction to influence resource supply between orgaizations and societies?

In sociology, a social organization is a pattern of relationship between and among individuals and social groups. Characteristics of social organization can include qualities, such as division of labour, communication system, leadership , structure of a organization. For hospital example, it is one social organization, whether how it uses its resource , it can inluence whether society has how much resources can use. Hospital is one social resource organization (division of labour), e.g. doctors, nurses teams, cleaner teams, patient customer enquire teams, counter service teams. They are a major influence on social behavior and is the link between human nature reaching to the hospital organizational and social environment. Hoe many actual patients number , social need in the year, if the year , there are not many patients need to feel to go to hospital , then it can influence the hospital feels resource excess, or it won't need to use more hospital resource to serve its patients in the year. S, social patients needs and hospital medicine supply needs, they have close relationship every year. It means that the hospital's medicine manufacture material won't need much, it the year has not many patients or patients number is decreasing. So, shopital organzation hoe to need its resource, it has close relationship to patients number in society (nature, demographic, economic, cultural and social behavior patterns and consciousness). So, it explains why the social organization is the best of all organized human society, such as hospital organization example, its patients number will influence medicine resource need.

Another example is bus public transport service social passengers number choice to catching bus transport tool, it can influence whether how buses use oil nature resources needs. If the year , there are less passengers to choose to catch buses, they choose to catch trams, trains, ferries in preference, then due to every bus reduces passengers numer, it does not often driven , following the fixed timetable. If the bus stations often have no many passengers are waiting buses, then many buses are often staying in bus stations. Consequently, bus oil fuel nature resources need must reduce. Thus, social bus passengers number may have indirect relationship to influence buses oil fuel natural resources needs every year. It means that bus oil fuel nature resource use amount is influened by social passengers public transport tool choice needs. It is one good example bus public transport service organization seems to be one social organization.

Ecommerce organization resource management strategy

Why does in this e-commerce organization situation, online webstore speed must be the most important factor to influence its sale success. Information technology internet speed, online webstore design, online transation convenience transaction feeling (tangibale and intangible both resource factors) may influence its future clients number ?

In behavioral economic view, any organizations must need to use resources to carry on any business or working activities. Resources may include:

management time to managements, working time to employees, information technology etc. office computer to administration, factory equipment to plant workers, plant or warehouse land space to logistic delivery or goods shelves, electricity, gas , water to workplace , even, employees number. HR to any department tasks. So, it seems that before any organization can finish any activities, they must need enough resources supply in order to satisfy any activities need. If the organization overall itself , even overall society. I shall explain as below:

For ecommerce organizatin example, any online trading firms must need to own high speed internet information technology resource to supply to any one technologic staff store to pay visa to buy any product in the most short time rapidly. So, its online store website speeds must need to be very fast in order to avoid to delay any country clients to carry on online transaction. If the ecommerce business organization can not support efficient, high speed internet service to let any countries online buyers to satisfy its online webstore purchase service. Then, any countries' online buyers may choose another online store to replace to buy its similar product easily.

Hence, convenient webstore online purchase service much be very important to influence this online webstore organization. It seems that technologic online internet resource must be the most influential factor to influence this online websore organization clients number. If its online website store can not supply rapid online purchase speed to let any one country to buy its products from its webstores rapidly. Then, its clients number may be influenced to reduce. So, in this e-commerce organization situation, online webstore speed must be the most important factor to influence its sale success. Information technology internet speed, online webstore design, online transation convenience transaction feeling (tangibale and intangible both resource factors) may influence its future clients number . So, judging whether the kind of resource is the most important to influence the organization's success, it depends on whether it needs to use what kind of resource to carry on its daily activities.

In fact, one organizational change has relationship to whether its reponses can have enough supply as well as its behavior can be influenced by the resources variable , the scarcity of any kinds of resources are supplied to be used. So, I believe that whether any kinds of resources are scarcity in the organizational environment, how much they are used, these any kind of resources can bring relationship to influence how organizational perceptions, interpretations and responses.

How an ecommerce organization resource affects society?
Why has online webstore's information technology resource close relationship t influence online buyers number and social job chance?

Organizational impact to the effect on an organization has any reponses to influence how on society chance. However, organizations can also have a positive impact on the economic satisfaction of a town. More oe less jobs supply to the wociety, which can be influenced by whether the organization can have effort to buy how much resources to be used in order to carry on itself any business activities. Hence, it seems that if the organization, such as the above online website sale product organization, if it can have enough money to employ web design professional to help it to design attractive website stores to let attract online buyer purchase choice, as well as paid higher internet service fee to improve its fee to improve its online internet speed in order to let any countries online customers can still click its website rapidly, even in busy online click time. Many people click computer mouse to enter ecommerce website stores in the same time. Then, any one won't choose another websites stores to replace its online sale service easily. Even, if it can buy many advanced computers to let its staffs can use the best quality computers to follow any client's ourchase transaction in short time. When , they confirm that whether the client's visa card payment can accept and what product he has paid to buy from its webstore. Then, the staff can know where the accurate address of the country , the client's product can be delivered rapidly. It will avoid to delay any product delivery. So, if this online store seller can have enough internet information technology source to support its whole computer information department staffs to wrk efficiently. Then, it can increase more online transaction chance in success. Consequently, it can grow up its online sale business, it will create many new potisition, due to its computer information technology dcpartmcnt must need to increase employees to help it to deal any countries online buyers online purchase service transactions and online product sale delivery service immediately in order to avoid online product delivery service to global online buyers. So, it can bring more job chance if this online webstore organization can have enough effort to buy high technological computer information products to let its online customer service staffs to use in order to improve online product delivery service store to let global many online buyers' attention . Consequently, it can apply online webstore purchase channel to apply website purchase channel to persuade many global online buyers online purchase choice to its webstore easily. So, it seems that this online webstore's information technology resource has close relationship t influence online buyers number and social job chance.

How do organizational resources affect organizational change?

IN general, resoults indicate that organizations possessing greater stocks of historically valuable resources were much less likely to engage in adaptive strategic change, but also that this resource-driven disinclination towards change tended to have a begin or even beneficial effect on performance . So, in general, if one organization lacks any one of these three important resources. It can influence this organization's performance to worse, they many include: human resource , financial resource, phycial resources and information resource. However, managers are responsible to acquiring and managing the resources to accomplish goals. If the organization can have enough resources to be used. It can bring positive impact to influence its overall organizational performance, even, when it has not any resource scarcity, it can avoid negative impacts on the society, such as increasing jobs chance. Hence, scarcity of capital, human and social resources to be provided to the organization, it will influence the organizational structure changes, even employee individual work attitude is influenced to change worse, when he/she can not have the best resources to be used in order to raise efficiency or improve performance more easily.

How to build organizatonal resource using right psychology

The psychology of management is the branch of psychology studying mental features of the person and its behavior in the course of planning, organization management and the control of joint activity. The human factor is considered as the central point in the psychology of management as its essence and a core. Hence , organizational psychology plays a very important rolw at the time or recruitment very important role at the time of recruitment taking disciplinary action or resolving disputes between employees. HR focus and expertise mainly lies in dealing with people . So , it makes sense that the study of the human mind, how to use organizational resources efficiently.

The organizational side of pschology is more focused on understanding how organizations affect individual behavior, organizational structures , social norms, management styles and role expectations are factors that can influence how people behave within organizations. In general, industrial organizational psychologists use psychological principles and research methods to solve problems in the workplace and improve the quality of life

(e.g. avoiding often waste industrial resources in manufacturing process aims). They study workplace workplace productivity and management and employee working styles. They get a feel for the morale and personality of a company or organization, e.g. suggesting to use skills and knowledge relating to psychology how to reduce same productivity level, but the organizational resources can be reduced to use. It is one kind the most efficiency resources using method to any kind of organizations.

On conclusion, industrial and organizational psychologists will often use science to study human behavior organizations and the workplaces. Their aims to help organizations to reduce excess resource using in any manufacturing process in order to reduce cost. Employers who need to attempt to learn how employees use resources to do work activities, it can bring these advanaages : learning how to use neuroscience to attract the right talent, retain high performing employees, because any organizations' resources will be used in order to manufacture any products or work activites by any employees in any time.

Employees are the ones who get the job done. They know how the organization and especially ho w their specigif team works best. So any one employee may be the important factor to influence the amount of resource use, any organizational resource use amount, it has close relationship to any employee work behavior. Moreover, resources, that is , group-level resources associated with shared relationship that foster a quality exchange of information and interaction between individuals within the workplace , helping any one employee to learn more about on the job training, use employee training optios to ensure department leader optimizes the employees' motiviation and potential retention. Aim to give opinions to employees to know how to avoid resource using waste method to achieve cost saving aim to the organization.

CHAPTER FIVE

OUTSOURCING SERVICE RESOURCE AVOIDS WASTE STRATEGY

Information Technology Outsourcing

In any organization information technology department, information system operations remain the predominant function outsourced, other functions are also being performed by external service providers and the relationship is between outsourcing and certain demographics: size, industry is formation intensity. The results suggest that system operations remain being performed by external service providers. Further, industry and information intensity has some influence on the extent of outsourcing of certain functions.

The first reason is cost reduction, trying to remain competitive and up-to-date is becoming a financial burden to many organizations. This is true particularly in fields, such as banking and financial services, health care and manufacturing. Hiring outsiders to handle part or even all of its information system often helps an organization to provide better services and maintain a competitive advantage. The information technology industry choice of outsourcing factor is related to size, industry type and information technology.

The second reason is technological and/or human resources in the management of the information technology infrastructure skill improvement. The information technology department outsourcing service to external service provider, includes the degree of internalization of technological resources and the degree of internalization of human resources. Some economists defined internalization of outsourcing service is as ownership is by the focal organization which takes on full control with profit and loss responsibility. Also who define outsourcing is as involving a significant use of resources, either technological and/or human resources, external to the organizational hierarchy in the management of the information technology infrastructure. So the information technology external service providers includes: applications development and maintenance, systems operations, networks/telecommunications management and user computing support, system planning and management purchase of application software, but excludes business consulting services, after-sale vendor services and the lease of telephone lines etc. outsourcing services.

The third reason is economics of scale in areas of hardware, software. This pressure is seen as the most significant factor driving today's corporate interest. An outsourcing service provision might be in a position to exploit economics of scale in areas of hardware, software and staff since it pools different kind of technological projects from many service receivers. Outsourcing information technological service can reduce the corporate's cost with the high level of IT investment, there are increasing pressures to move away from fixed expenditure, corporate overhead towards a more direct variable cost approach to control the IT operations. The IT costs can become predictable for overruns is often placed on the service provider. Outsourcing service can allow the service to gain immediate access to competitiveness in delivering products or services as well as to avoid of obsolescence risk, due to the changes in the nature of the IT infrastructure, the risk of obsolescence is high. Outsourcing can allow the service provider has the ability to diversify these risks across a broad range of service receivers. However, long term contracts might in spread the risk, the weakness is back to the receiver.

It seems outsourcing IT service has also these disadvantages: such as, loss of flexibility or managerial control. Outsourcing reduces real or perceived control over both quality real or perceived control over both the quality of software and the timetable of project since the work is now being carried out by people not under direct supervision. It also threats to long term career prospects to information system professionals because many of them do not find suitable. Is jobs or promising career paths in both areas of the corporation. Outsourcing also increases coordination cost. It may requires increasing time to communicate and coordinate with the service provider. Traditionally, the formal meeting cost of negotiating and monitoring the outsourcing contract are potentially wide ranging, indirect and substantial increasing, such as, additional releasing or transferring employees, in license transfer by software vendors and in re-negotiating contracts costs. So, the IT industry of profit motivates service provider might not be in the least interests of the outsourcing service receivers. Some IT service providers are in the business of maximizing their profit at any cost, this could run counter to a service receiver's interest.

●

Outsourcing or insourcing in human resource supply chain factor

To choosing of outsourcing or insourcing in human resource supply chain factor of the controlling service demanders needs to concern this issues: Should human resource activities be provided in house or should all or past of those activities be outsourced? The relationship between organizational structure and the HR function is an important variable. The individual activities that comprise HR systems include not only the employee life cycle from recruiting to termination, but also planning for organizational staffing needs and improving organizational effectiveness. How organizations need to outsource HR function to not care employees knowledge and skill is a factor to influence any organizations choose to outsourcing non core employees when which have no any right employees to be promoted to do the position. For example, firms engage in HR outsourcing to reduce management access HR expertise, achieve workforce flexibility, focus managerial resources and keep up with changing workplace negotiations. Also, supporting the tend is the availability of common technology platform, which can reduce costs for organizations and risks. However, organizations are afraid of losing some control over delivery of outsourcing services and finding themselves dependent on the vendor or liable for the vendors actions where there are both benefits and challenges may be informed by the structure of the relationship between client firms and these organizations offering the outsourced activities to client firms.

What variables are impacted by HR outsourcing of staffing? Which include: administrative costs for labor expense, client firm to HR relations, HR regulatory competency requirement, knowledge of cost factors, e.g. billing and pay rates, vendor markups and margins, vendor management competency requirement, client and vendor relationship, communication is between client managers and staffing vendor, employee data-available, data quality control, data security, match with job requirement, employee quality, inter-vendor competition, mining of client talent by vendor , quality content for preferred staffing vendor, standardization of business process (intra-company), strategic focus of client firm, demands on client managers vendor competency and external economic environmental viability.

However, it has dynamic relationship between the client firms and staffing vendors. Moreover, the models of human resource supply chain, every has different set of advantages and disadvantages for the client firms. The models can be relate to the decision making process on outsourcing of human resources. As strategic services tactic decisions have an important impact or selecting the particular HR outsourcing model that a client firm adopter. The another model is the balance of power and control over managing the control workers differ to decide what every worker individual skills or abilities outsourcing demand. Moreover, local contracting is also the predominant traditional model for outsourcing staffing with non-core employees. A client firm usually uses several staffing vendors to meet temporary staffing needs for seasonal functions, employee absences and special projects. The advantages of local contracting are high touch and high quality of service by staffing vendors, minimal bureaucracy, empowerment of hiring any high qualified employees to get the job done, and a relatively better fit between specific staffing vendors and functional needs.

The disadvantages of local contracting can increase costs from non-standardization of hiring practices and procedures across the client form, a significant amount of word of mouth and subjective quality issues, high local costs and client firm us subjected to the capabilities of the staffing vendors and contract employees. However, local HR contracting is the most flexible, high quality, but expense, inefficient and ineffective HR outsourcing model for the client firm. Another model is the working period to be decided to outsource HR contracting. In this situation, in the short term and on a day-to-day basis, the client firm aims to achieve on economy of scale with its staffing vendors. The total costs of temporary workers as well as internal costs for contracting with several different vendors are higher than if it needs one staffing vendors to meet all its needs. So, the client company can set the reasonable pricing that it pays for its temporary outsourcing staffs. Each staffing vendor secures a different rate range with each vendor as opposed as one contact. In the long term, it is benefiting, each specialized staffing vendor is able to fully work with each function needs temporary utilization is better than the average. Mismatches are fewer. Functional departments are able to receive a high quality / high touch service in any time period. Another model is the centralizing is when the department standardizes the staffing process to drive costs down of temporary workers. This tends to occur when a percentage of non-core employees reach a certain ratio of core employees. The advantages include more uniform standards in hiring process, billing rates and pay rates, departmental hiring managers can refocus their effort to choose outsourcing staffing, criteria may be established for a performed suppliers list and greater security for the staffing established vendors that offer higher quality services. The disadvantages include new departmental responsibilities in HR which decreases outsourcing efficiencies for the organizations daily administrative direction is rather than long term strategic direction. Usually lacking qualifications to fulfill the responsibilities, overall, centralizing of HR outsourcing is that firms can achieve more standardization which additional bureaucratic costs and the necessary non-core jobs do not get done as a need. Another model is purchasing HR, which manages staffing vendors from HR to the purchasing unit of an organizations. The goal is to continue cost reductions by increasing efficiencies. In conclusion, the main benefits of HR outsourcing include maintaining organizational control over the hiring process, application of purchasing capabilities for greater standardization in hiring processes pay rates and bill rates. So, any outsoucred HR organizations may be reduce hiring process cost.

●

Global outsourcing source strategy
in a value supply chain

What is global outsourcing source strategy in a departmental role? In a highly competitive global environment, many manufacturers are responded by setting and outsourcing relations for components and finished products with lower cost producers on a contractual electronic commerce department, (original equipment manufacturer basis). Outsourcing strategy is part of the value supply chain of corporate activated. Nowadays, global outsourcing increases organizational and technological capacity of firms and cooperating a network of remotely located external suppliers performing. These understanding the important roles that product designers, engineers and production managers and purchasing manager etc. play in global sourcing strategy empowerment. Specially, electronic commerce is popular to supply chain. For example, Toyota car manufacturing company, owns unique capabilities by designing and manufacturing certain car components in-house , i.e. insourcing. Toyota also outsource manufacturing activities, Toyota adopts purchasing necessary, but no strategic inputs from independent component suppliers on obtaining a lower cost for these inputs. For example, products would be belts, tires and batteries to vehicle products that are not customized and do not differentiate its products from its competitors. Toyota's outsourcing strategy is car strategic inputs provide differentiation, e.g. engine, transmission etc. are sources from suppliers based on strategic partnership to gain to access to suppliers' capabilities and it is also a conceptualize global outsourcing sourcing strategy to Toyota car manufacturing company.

How value chain outsourcing affects firm level performance. Global outsourcing strategy means to identify which production units that will serve which particular markets and how components will be supplied for production and thus included a number of basic choices, companies can make in decision how to serve various markets. Either choice relates to the use of inputs, assembly or production within the country to serve a foreign market or decides to use of internal or external supplies of components or finished products. In this outsourcing source input situation, the term sourcing is needed to describe how multi-national companies mange in of components and finished products in serving foreign and domestic markets. Sourcing decision making is both contractual point of view, the sourcing of major components and products are occurred by multi-national companies. First is from parents or their foreign subsidiaries. Second is from independent suppliers on a contractual basis. The first type of sourcing is known as insourcing. Otherwise, the second type of sourcing is referred to outsourcing. How to achieve economies of scale by outsourcing or insourcing sourcing input strategy? Therefore, the two outsourcing strategies are multi-faceted and require careful examination.

●

Outsourcing benefits in economic view

The two economists (Abrahamson & Rosenkopf, 1993) indicated that In long term, outsourcing can help to reduce fixed investment in finance view point, in-house manufacturing facilities and thus lower the breakeven point, which subsequently helps boost an outsourcing company whose return on equity (ROE). Thus, if any one corporate performance is evaluated on the basis of its contribution to the company's ROE. Also, in the short term or long term on resource inputs outsourcing view, early adopters of outsourcing strategy indeed experienced efficiency gains as they were able to reduce fixed investment in in-house manufacturing facilities and lows their ROE. But, later adopters may have different to gain institutions legitimacy or because of competition pressures in the industry, despite some inherent uncertainties about the long term costs and benefits of outsourcing strategy. It seems that outsourcing strategy was devised as any organization's policy makers to access trade linkages of benefits for short term or long term. Outsourcing strategy is a systematic analysis of the economic, political and regulatory implications indicates potential benefits along with a number of potentially negative side effects to any organizations. Then, outsourcing strategy will be caused this question: How to assess the risks and benefits of outsourcing for organizational sectors and nations both? The decision to change outsourcing behavior to carry a business activity may have profound implications for outsourcer and outsource receiver both, but little impact of the sector level. The common occurrence of industry decisions to outsource most manufacturing, including sale of factories, it created a new sub-sector, contract manufacturing. Otherwise, at a national level and public sectors become less distinct to outsourcing strategy. Public policy on outsourcing has stimulated extensive debate, privatization social justice and value for money etc. challenges.

●

What motivate outsourcing what is being outsourced risk and concerns?

Whether what motivate outsourcing, evidence of what is being outsourced risk and concerns? Outsourcing activities include: outsources manufacturing components and other value adding activities. Some focused on employment is outsourced another firm's employees carrying out tasks previously performed one's own employees. Outsourcing is an activity outside the organization's chosen core competencies. It seems outsourcing is a sub-contracting relationships between firms, all foreign production, hiring of workers in non-traditional jobs, such as control workers and temporary and part time workers.

What are the motivations for outsourcing reasons? Why outsourcing is needed to any organization. For example, it can enable firms to focus on core activities. The concept of focus originates in operation on a small, manageable, number of tasks at which the operation becomes excellent to specific technologies and as a risk of vertical integration advantages. Other benefits of outsourcing appear is literature on strategic management, operations management, purchasing and supply and innovations. Moreover, outsourcing can improve flexibility to meet changing business conditions, demands for products, services and technologies by creating smaller and more flexible clear evidence includes improved creditability image, greater workforce flexibility and avoiding being backed into specific assets and technologies are harder to measure. How outsourcing can improve company performance. For airline manufacturing industry example, Hill & Jones (1995) showed that the manufacture of a large portion of the Boeing 767 is Boeing's third largest commercial aircraft, which is outsourced to Japanese manufacturers, which include Fuji, Kawasaki and Mitsubish. As a result, only 10% of the value of the 767 Boeing is produced in-house. So, outsourcing is an attempt to enhance manufacturing air place industry competitiveness.

●

How can choose smarter outsourcing?

How can choose smarter outsourcing? Organizations hope to do sight options to save money, among themselves staff layoffs and a reduction of overhead costs, such as office space. Private companies have long outsourced in order to save time and money. During periods of economic growth, many organizations began to use outsourcing more frequently and staff workloads grew in proportion to increase budgets. Tasks such as conducting needs assessments, reviewing proposals, conducting site visits, monitoring and creating evaluations systems were increasingly given to outside contractors, consulting firms and independent consultants in the belief that external specialists could do the work more efficiently and effectively than company itself.

Nowadays, there is a growing stream of organizations need to research into the outsourcing of innovation activities within the innovation, management, marketing and economics disciplines. These organizations need to understand how with the outsourcing practice becoming more commonplace in their industry. However, their behaviors bring these two questions: Whether outsource or internalize innovation activities and the performance implications of this decision can support for both transaction cost and resource based arguments is examined with both theory bases showing substantial attention? Whether outsourcing innovation activities can lead to faster product development and cost savings? On advantages hand, it is possible that outsourcing may lead to higher costs and slower new product development. Further the technological uncertainty may have conflicting impacts on the outsourcing decision that are not yet well understand. When outsourcing product development has reduced costs and has proved speed to market. On disadvantages hand, outsourcing has also reduce product development time delays and higher quality concerns. Why to cause performance implications of outsourced innovation activities in transaction in cost economics and the resource-based view point? When outsourcing product development has been to reduce costs and has improved speed to market, outsourcing product development is not unlike other make or buy decisions. So, make vs buy decision is similar to logistic and IT outsourcing. Internalization of product development will be preferred when transaction costs are excessive. Otherwise, the market i.e. outsourcing will be selected when transaction costs are low. Transaction costs can include adaption, safeguarding and measurement costs. Adaption costs represent efforts to adjust contract to change conditions and are a result of environmental uncertainty. When a firm may have to revise on agreement with a partner company, this facing substantial penalties, due to an unstable market environments, the firm is likely to perform this function internally. Safeguarding costs characterize the costs of an outsourcing provider acting opportunities after investments have been made in the inter-firm relationship and are the result of transaction specific investment. Measurement costs include all expenses with confirming that contracts have been fulfilled passably. The contracting firm may face substantial costs to estimate quality for contractual services. When the sum total of these transaction costs is substantial, internalization will be favored.

●

What is environmental uncertainty factor?

Environmental uncertainty refers to unanticipated changes in circumstances surrounding an exchange in market uncertain and technological uncertainty. Market uncertainty is the fluctuation and unpredictability of demand. With respect to innovation projects, market uncertainty may cause frequent changes to the development, complications and adding expense to external contracting. These changes may necessitate renegotiation or cancellation of innovation contracts, which will likely carry prohibitive penalties (a term) transaction costs. These transaction costs promote internalization under high levels of market uncertainty. Otherwise, technological uncertainty environments, selecting market governance allows firms the flexibility to end relationship should technical requirements shift. It seems that market and technological external change factor will influence to benefits to any organizations to choose outsourcing strategy. On the other side, outsourcing can bring this question: Whether the offshore outsourcing of information technology jobs choice is suitable to any IT organizations? Nowadays. The offshore outsourcing if IT jobs from the United States has been enabled by a powerful influence of global economic demographic and technological forces. In fact, many IT companies were drawn to offshoring outsourcing because of the need for programmers to fix the Y2K problem in the late 1990- year. It is shortages of US programmers. Other factors driving this phenomenon include the wage gap between the US and developing countries, e.g. China and India, advances in technology, labor availability, expanding foreign markets and foreign government incentives. The spread of the offshoring phenomenon from low skill manufacturing to high wage white collar service industry jobs reduces the country's IT jobs critics, it represents the mobility for many US workers who saw post-secondary education as the route to a higher standard of living. The offshoring outsourcing of manufacturing and service jobs from the US to lower cost foreign nations become a national issue in a very short time. The impact of offshore outsource on the information technology sector gives outsourcing potential loss of millions of jobs at all wage levels and the critical contribution is the IT sector to US productivity growth. However, decisions about the locations of manufacturing or service facilities reflect market forces key factors include the size of local markets, capital availability and costs, labor availability skill levels and cost, logistic issues, reliability and infrastructure and IT in particular relationships with research institutions. All these factors will influence the choice of offshore outsource IT jobs strategy top any organizations.

●

Whether outsourcing will bring
what kind of work skills.

Whether outsourcing will bring what kind of work skills. Many employers choose outsourcing to employ employees. This core of our work is identifying trends which will transform global society and the global marketplace. How it influences our nature of work form health care to technology, the work place and human identity. A decade ago, workers worried about jobs being outsourced overseas. Today companies, such as Odesk and Liveops can assemble teams " in the cloud" to dosales, customer support and many other tasks. It seems outsoucring can influence many high technological job of changes. Global connectivity, smart machines and new media are just some of the drivers reshaping how we thank about work, what constitutes work and the skills, we shall need to be productive contributors in the future. As computer technology in the cloud will be used popularly to society. A signal is typically a small or local innovation that has the potenial to grow in scale and geographic distribution. A signal can be a new product, a new practice, a new market strategy, a new policy or new technology, such as online cloud computing files storage service method. It is an innovative social science method to computer users. However, this new computer files storage method influences outsourcing service of needs increasing. It will have key drivers and skills areas that will be most relevant to the technological workforce of the future.

It is estimates that by 2025 year, the number of Americans over 60 age will increase by 70%. The challenge of an aging population will come. What it means to age, individuals will need to rearrange their approach to their career, family life and education to accommodate their life plan. Increasing, people will work long past 65 age in order to have adequate resources for retirement. Multiple careers will be commplace and lifelong learning to prepare for occupational change will see major growth. To take advantage of this well experienced organizations will have to rethink the traditional career paths in organizations, creating more diversity and flexibility. As the high technological cloud computing storage method is invented. Any organizations can save their files to the central cloud computer storage system website to save or find their files from website more easily. It will reduce their computer department expenditure and staff salary. So, outsourcing computer file storage service demands will be influenced to increase to any organizations as well as organizations will reorganize their computer department job nature to shape the kinds of social, economic and political organizations which inhabit. Outsourcing is a good solve method to assist organizations to pay cheap salary to employ many retired high age workers by contract or temporary or part time method to reduce their computer department's number of employees and the retired labors only need to pay cheap salary to learn how to use internet to help whose employers to save their files to their outsourcing computer storage service provider's central computer storage system every day efficiently. So, organizations do not need to employ many computer department staffs to avoid to pay much salaries to this computer department expenditure. They can choose outsourcing to pay cheap salaries to employ many retirement labors to assist them to do simple office storage job from internet channel efficiently and effectively. Hence, internet high technological innovation can influence office outsoucing of job duties increasing.

Whether domestic outsoucing in the America, what assesses trends and effects on job quality. Nowadays, US firms' use of contractors and independent contractors and its effect on job quality and inequality. Why firms choose contract out for certain functions and assess their predictions about likely impacts on job quality, stagnant wages, growing inquality and the deterioration of job quality are among the most important challenges facing the US economy today. Although any country's domestic outsourcing , firms' use of contractors, franchises and independent contractors any one of these factors is a potentially important influence to companies reduce compensation and shift economy risk to workers. However, the domestic outsoucing takes place on a much larger scale and effects many more workers than has been recognized ranging from low wage service workers, security guards, warehouse workers and hotel housekeepers to professionals and technical workers, such as programmers, health care technicians and accountants. These tends are part of structural change in the organization of production to influence quality of jobs and the nature of employment contract after outsourcing jobs are popular. The quality of jobs include wages, benefits, employee skills and training and mobility opportunities and job security as well as inequality across jobs. Domestic outsoucing concerns these issues: such as employment and labor law, the provision of health, pension and other workplace benefits. However, any companies choose outsourcing of employment reasons include, such as that it relates how management choices to pursue value added or cost focused strategies. Contracting out is difficult to define because a large part ot economic activity has always occurred through business-to-business transactions, as captured in macro-economic input-output models. Outsoucing job employment method can influence any one labor's individual quality of jobs. Usually, international companies choose the offshoring of work in global supply chains. Until recently, the domestic counterpart outsourcing employment method has grown supply chains to domestic or regional outsoucing employment.

What factors cause domestic outsourcing and whether firm decisions about what to retain in-house and what to outsource have changes over time. Some evidence suggests that firms have responded by focusing on their core competencies and outsourcing low value added tasks as well as higher value added specialized functions. Advanced technologies have facilitated this process by allowing firms to outsource entire functions ans more easily monitor contractors as well as employees who work, leading to new forms of networked production and rise of specialized outsouring employment firms. Domestic outsoucing influences the changes of job quality, benefits, hours, workload, job stability, schedule stability and occupational safety, health, incidence of wage theft and access to training and promotions. Predictions are less clear for job requiring professional or technicial or specialized skills or those that are outsourced to large and diversified outsourced contractors. Types of outsourced contracts include: suppliers or vendors of products, such as manufacturing inputs or services, such as business services or staffs service or staffing firms, franchisees and independent contract, such as freelancers, independent contracts or non demand platform outsourced workers. It is significant restructuring of domestic manufacturing supply chains will greater reliance on suppliers and subcontractors. In addition, the potential growth of on demand outsourcing work as well as other forms of job fragmentation. It causes this question: How outsourced workers are multiple forms of income generating work to achieve economic security and how outsourcing workers can build career across jobs and over time.

Firm in every sector of the economy contract with other firms as part of their production process, as do governmental entities. The functions that are outsourced vary widely. For example: human resources ans research and development functions, building services, recycling, regulation and compliance, accounting, credit card collection, call centres, mortage and check processing, information technology and data processing, logistics and transportation, machine maintenance, cable installation, food services, food processing, parts manufacturing and assembly, laundry and housekeeping etc. outsourced jobs causes.

Whether what business impact of outsourcing will be caused? Nowadays, IT outsourcing was clearly a part of an effective management strategy that the companies felt IT outsourcing strategy can bring to achieve positive results. Information technology outsourcing providing servicers will be predicted to provide services that is expected to raise over the next five years minimum. The companies demand clients expected benefits of IT outsourcing and determined that cost reduction, increased operation, efficiency and improved IT effectiveness. What are the impacts of outsourcing to influence better long-term improvement in the business performance? It is impossible to being benefits of significant reduction and lower growth in sellings, general and administrative expense to IT outsourcing company demand clients. Also, pre-existing corporate cultures are focused on business improvement to IT outsourcing company demand clietns. In the past researches, some economists indicated that points can be used to reflect the actual numbers increase or decrease in percent. However, their prior researches shows that prior to outsourcing, the annual growth in selling, general and administration expenses of eompanies in the study was already 4.2 points lower than sector medium. Moreover, within one to two years after IT outsourcing these companies improved even most. Annual growth in selling and general administrative expenses for them was 9.9 points lower efford to assist any IT outsourcing will have selling and administrative expenses for long term. Also, almost two-third of the companies studied outperformed in increased growth in return on asset two to three years after IT outsourcing commenced. Prior to outsourcing, the annual ROA growth rate for companies in the study ws 7.5 points lower than the sector median. After outsourcing, however these companies experienced 8.6 points higher median a substantial change of 16.1 points. Also, nearly two to third of the companies studied grew earnings faster than their peers. Two to three years after IT outsourcing, companies experienced an annual rate of growth in earnings 11.8 points higher than the growth rate of the sector median. Thus, it seems IT outsourcing can assist the IT outsourcing demand clients to reduce expenditure and to raise income both as the same time. Then, it will cause these questions to IT outsourcing demand clients. Is outsourcing influencing in an economic downturn to finance sector in the short term? Is the finance sector's renewed change for outsourcing just a temporary cost-cutting measure? Will today's economic climate initiate long term financial and productivity gains? Whether what are benefits and disadvantages of outsourcing finance sector IT. I shall demonstrate why outsourcing open source software support and maintenance can be a good choice to start. Firstly when company plans to budget cuts expenditures, IT outsourcing is often the first choice. For example in 2003 year, Zurich Financial services' sprawling IT department consisted of more than 7,500 employees. After posting a record loss of 3.4 billion the year before, Zurich decided to cut down on in those staff and outsource nearly half of its IT work. Outsourcing has successfully cut costs by 45 percent and cut the number of in house IT staff by 60 percent. Here are some of the benefits that companies enjoy when they outsource information technology functions to competent, reliable vendors.

In fact, it can be too expensive to maintain, company's own information technology, especially during a recession. Fortunately, many IT functions can be easily and efficiently outsourced, positively impacting individual company's bottom line. Employee costs are much higher than just salary and benefits, keeping employees happy, productive and busy takes time, effort and money. Although, many IT staffs will be dismissed, it will increase the unemployment ratio in societies. But, moving an IT service out of house means financial organizations don't have to worry about technology refresh costs in the future. It also cuts down on human resources requirements, specialist IT service provides which can provide the newest technologies and deliver quality service more than company itself in house information provides are the most effective to develop and implement and upgrade their clients' software or the launch on a new platform, due to the expert's time is wasted on day-to-day duties for whose other IT outsourcing demand clients. However, instead of IT outsourcing service outsourced offshoring in that service sector, how economic impact to influence the outsourced offshoring country. For example, United States continues to run an international trade surplus in services. Many Americans are particularly concerned about the loss of skilled, well paid jobs in such fields as computer programming and accounting etc. positions. These jobs seemed relatively secure at a time when many manufacturing jobs were being cost to import competition. Similarly, telephone call centers, once viewed as an esonomic development opportunity in some areas, increasingly are moving low wage countries, such as India and the Philippines. Thus, offshoring raises many questions for policymakers and general public. For example, which service jobs will be affected most by import competition. What are the likely effects of service-sector offshoring on U.S.A. output, employment and our standard of living, such as America? Is offshoring really a problem that requires restrictive government actions or are other kinds of policies more appropriate to give Americans or other countries the highest possible living standard?

The term of offshoring refers to the relocation of jobs and production to a foreign country. The relocated jobs and production could be at a foreign office of the same multinational company or at a separate company located abroad. In constrast, the term outsourcing doesn't necessary imply that jobs and production are relocated to another country. The major outsourcing service jobs include human resource, accounting and information technology etc. in-house service jobs in large organizations. However, the loss of service jobs and factory production is caused by offshoring is diffuclt to measure. It is also difficult to determine the impact of offshoring on total services employment in the United States or other countries. International trade in services covers a wide range of industries and activites. For example, travel and transportation includes travel expenditures, passenger fares and frieght and port services, royalties and license fees cover transactions including patents, copyrights, trademarks and other intangible proprietary rights to use, produce or distribute products. Other private services include many of these industries, such as education, financial services insurance, telecommunications and other professional services etc. Some economists indicated that occupational employment statistics for the Unisted States provided additional evidence that past service sector offshoring had been small. About 14 million service jobs were at risk of offshoring in 2000 year, when about 96 million service jobs had a low risk of ofshoring. The decline in the at-risk service occupations from 2000 year to 2002 year was about 218,000 jobs or roughly 109,000 jobs annually, relatively small number that is consistent with the estimates of McCarthy or Zandi. In percentage terms, employment in the at risk occupations fell at a faster rate from 2000 year to 2002 year than in the low risk occupations.

This faster decline is consistent with offshoring activity, although the decline is consistent with other explanations as well, such as faster of technological change in industries employing the risk occupations or greater cyclical sensitivity in these industries. Because offshoring was not the only cause of job loss in the risk occupations, the number of jobs moved offshore was undoubtedly less than 109,000 jobs annually. However, the estimates may understate the total impact because domestic companies with expanding worldwide employment may have located may of their newly created jobs abroad even when they didn't reduce their US employment. Some of those foreign jobs might provide services to US customers and potentially foreign jobs might provide service to US . Conversely, the estimates may overstate the total job loss from offshoring of the foreign outsourcing of some support jobs prevents the loss of other domestic jobs by keeping US firms competitive in world markets. For example, cost reductions from offshoring IT jobs might help a US financial services company win foreign contracts, preserving many professionals and support jobs in the US.

Lower production costs in foreign countries are a major cause of service sector offering. Although, the costs of land and other resources may be cheaper abroad, but the main difference betweeb the US and developing countries is labor costs. There is a large gap in computer programmer wages between the US and other countries. Any organizational capital includes both physical capital, such as machinery and computers and human capital , such as skills and knowledge. The cost savings is come from offshoring also might be reduced if the firm needed to pay higher transportation and telecommunication costs or management spends more time on service quality and data security. Still, the much lower levels of wages ans benefits in developing countries suggests that many services can be produced abroad at lower cost. The in-house professional relocation of labor-intensive service activities, such as legal transcription services to countries with lower labor costs is consistent with economists' basic theory of international trade, comparative advantage. So, in-house outsourced professional service will be a corporative advantage, if the country's legal profession is poor level to compare with the another country. e.g. the skill in-house the legal professional labors of the developing country, such as China is poor educational level to compare with the developed country, such as US. So, if China large organizations chose to outsource themselves in-house legal service jobs to outsource offshoring to US legal professional lawyers to do. It can bring comparative advantage to China large outsourced in-house legal service organizations, due to these China outsourced large organizations can reduce to employ to pay too much salaries to these many in-house Chinese domestic lawyers and the US outsourced legal consultants whose can give more professional legal recommendation to serve to the China large organizations.

In conclusion, although offshoring strategy can increase unemployment chance for this disadvantge. But, all of outsourcing benefits weighs are more than the offsourcing disadvantages. However, outsourcing strategy can have these benefits to the outsourced service demanders. Such as outsourcing is no longer just about cost saving, it is also a strategic tool that may power the twenty first century global economy. Moreover, outsourcing can increase productivity and competitiveness, e.g. for every 1000 jobs British Airways sends to India , the airline saves $23 million, companies can devote a portion of their outsourcing savings to helping employees make job transitions, also leader can no longer afford to view outsourcing as a business tactic, it is now essential to remain competitive. On the world stage, workers now compete globally, so individuals must continually learn more to vie successfully with their peers worldwide, the average company only spends about 20% of the value of its outsourcing contracts to manage its relationship with the outsource provider. So, in the positive view point, outsourcing strategy can bring a potential primary driver of the global economy development. Although, outsourcing can also cause the raising of domestic unemployment chance. But companies may soon be more outsourced than in sourced, signifying a fundamental reorganization that will affect employees, managers, customers and executives. Customers' choice will increase product costs will drop and workers' roles will change. Finally, the most important, the developing country will earn comparative advantage from the developed country's employers' offshoring jobs provision. Thus, the developing country's unemployment rate will be reduced, then the global economy will be kept more balance fairly.

Reference
Abrahamson, E., & Rosenkopf., (1993). Institutional and competitive bandwagons: Using mathematical
modeling and a tool to explore innovation diffusion.
　　Academy of management review, 18(3), 487-517.
Hill, C.W.L. & Jones, G.R. 1995. Strategic management, An integrated

approach. Boston: Houghtom Mif In.

Robots whether can help organizations to avoid resource waste

To judge whether robots can help any organizations to avoid resources waste behavior. We need to know whether robots can own recyle function. How do robots helpthe environment? Robots can help reduce waste that is implemented by effectively sorting materials that can be recycled and put to use again. They can even help sort waste materials quickly and move efficiently than humans reduce the input power amd cost unsociated with such processes. However, robots also may help business organizations with recycling, instead of natural environment . For example, tobots may help organization facility cut operate resource cost and allowed to take on a second load of recyclables to sort throgh.

How robotic technology help organizations reduce waste?

Advanced software has made it easier to plan out routes that can efficiently guide waste collecting the waste and recycling materials that need to be collected. It also makes collection more fuel efficient and reduces energy usage to any offices, plants, warehouses, business organizations. It seems that robots can help organizations to bring recycling advantages. We should definitely keep on teaching robots to recycle our waste, e.g. clean robotics makes waste management smart with a robotic trash can that automatically separates used and not used materials in workplace environment.

How to use technology to help reduce waste?

There is no financial incentive to reduce waste. One of a few manufacturers of AI (arificial intelligence) powered recycling robots. We can imagine a future where waste-collectig robots will move through air land, and water, cleaning our natural environment, workplace environment conveniently. For example, now robots are being put on duty to help solve the environment pollution, material waste, recycling challenges. AI assisted robotis technology that can work with humans in workplace organizational environment to have robots to do a better job at sorting garbage and reduce the building materials is wasted, sorting trash is a dirty and dangerous job, recycling robots may help human to do thin kind of sorting trash job, even further atomic bombs soon could be delivered over intercontinental distances aboard " pick a back" multi-stage rockets by robotis assistance. So, in our future, robotic can be applied on those avoiding resource waste job aspects, such as degradation and resource depletion , reduce , reuse, recycle and recover, have always been needed to avoid resource waste to future global business organizations. When, AI machine learning and robotics could help us , more efficiently organization, digital tools and new business models.

How green robots are helping with environmental sustainablity?

Robots can help reduce waste that is implemented by effciently sorting materials that can be recycled and put to use again. They can even help sort waste materials quickly and most efficiently than humans reducing the input power and cost associated with such processes.

How robots may help organizations to avoid resource waste?

Waste robotics autonomous recycling technology integrates advanced waste technology to avoid the costly deployment to any organizational users, e.g. the clean sea robot is an autonomous, electric floating aqua-droue that sweeps and collects plastic trash that has collected in coastal areas. It uses a has collected in coastal areas . It uses a combination of computer vision and remote sensing basd on 3D laser scanning technologies . So, clean sea robots can bring sea environmental protection advantages to global seas. Future global sea environment protection organization must need its clean sea tasks helping.

Instead of clean sea rubbish aspect, robots can also help organizations to do digital waste management tasks, digital technologies and their current use in waste management transparent, more economic and more resource-efficient processes, better souring of current important robotis digital waste manaement, technological trends, are robotics,the internet of things, cloud, digital rubbish robotic can help organizations to reduce digital rubbsh easily. then, any organizational digital system can do more efficient tasks daily. Hence, robotics can help e-commerce organizations to do digital resource waste management tasks in order to provide high efficient online purchase services to any countries online buyers in short time.

How robots are applied to reduce waste in hotel organizations?

Reducing waste in hotels in within reach with the help of digital technologies. How are robots used in hotels? Throughout the hotels, robots are deployed to provide information, front desk services, storeage services as well as check in and cleck out services , with technology including voice and facial recognition. An example, of artifical intelligence in the hospitality industry is the use of AI to deliver in-person customer service. The robot is able to provide tourist information to customers who interact with it. Most impressively, it is able to learn from human speech and adapt to individuals. waste management in hotels is important or it is getting increasingly difficult to dispose of waste. Therefore, hotel resource management robots can help hotels to decrease cost of waste disposal as the start with: Using refillable dispensers for soaps, shampoos and conditioners. Could hotel service robots help the hospitality industry on resource management of robotized hotels, e.g. avoding food waste in hotel robotized hotels, example restaurants robotics technology can help chefs measure, manage and reduce food wase. Morevoer, a restuaurant robots do not get waste and can perform to help chels measure, manage and reduce food waste easily. From a human resource management point of view, in that sense, robotisation may help automation and hotels to improve it service and reduce restaurant food waste cost.

Management science role solves
resources shortages

● What does management resource science mean ?

Although, management science could include the study of all activities of groups that means a management function, it generally include discovering, developing, defining and evaluating the goals of the organization and alternative policies that will lead towards the goals. So, management science is the broad interdisiplianary study of problem solving and decision making in human organizations with strong links to management economics, business , engineering , management consulting fields. Management science helps business to achieve golas using of organizational resources to produce goods and service. It is a contemporary approach to management that is an extension of scientific management that measures the worker to task mix and ratio to raise efficiency.

Thus, the nature of management science is a science because it contains a systematic body of knowledge in the form of general principles. Management principles are important in nature, but they can not be expected to give same results in every suitation. Therefore, management is a social science. If any organizations feel resources are shortages, they need to find that the main factors to influence their resources are often shortage. Management science may be one kind the best management research choice, because it uses various scientific research-based principles, strategies and analytical methods including mathematical modeling, statistics and numerical methods to improve an organization's ability to enact rational and accurate management decisions by arriving at optional or near oprimal solutions to complex decision.

● Why does management science help organizations to avoid/solve resource shortage?

Because management is a core function of every business and a number of theories try to explain how any why resource will be use rapidly and resource shortage causes to any organization. The core function of the management science approach is to compare possible outcomes. In addition, managers in various functions have aware of the potential contribution of analytical modes . So, the managerical science function involves arranging equipment perform functions, such as procurement, production etc. activities.

For drug manufacturing organization or hospital, clinic, medical service organizations exmaple, any kinds of drug must be important resource to provide patients to eat. If they have not enough drugs to be provided to the hospital, clinic, medical service organizational patients to eat. Then, their sicknesses may become serious suddenly. So, managing enough drugs stick is very important. However, management science may help any one these medical organization to implement rationality in strategic decisions: Choice which kinds of drugs purchase number, in order to keep enough drugs supply in drug store room. Understanding in a drug resource pool choice, due to cash available is limited to any one medical organizations.

Management science aims to avoid drug shortage to any one medical organizations. Such as this drug organization case, management science may help them to identify the processes, which kinds of drugs are needed to buy immediately, notice the areas of weaknesses, and realize the future possibilities and needs of the medical organization's patient customers needs. The approach makes the drug utilization of resources easier, since the framework can notice the availability of drug resources and the proper eat of them to be provided to any sickness kinds of patients to eat immediately when the medical organization can have enough drug stocks supply.

How to apply management science to help hospital better prepare for a drug shortage management method may include: Having a plan, the director of pharmacy should consider developing a plan for managing drug shortages, implement structured communications. Ask the right questions,instead of , hospital management also needs to know what is causing drug shortages. IN fact, drug shortages are caused by many factors, including: regulatory issues, and business decisions as well as many other disturbances within the supply chain.

Hence, in management science view point, hospital can attempt to apply mobile App technolgies tool to solve drug shortage problem, because mobile App technologies tool can be one kind of immediate communication tool, it can identify when the kind of drug will shortage and their impact on hospitals, e.g. how many the kind of sickness patient number and automates the entire life cycle of managing any kinds of drug shortage. Mobile App, communication technologic tool can provide clinical information that allows teams to understand and mitigate the ramifications for shorted medications. Any possible drug shortage solution in hoepital, it may be a management strategy that includes clear policies and producers for information. It defines a drug shortage is as a supply issue that affects how the drug store room's daily drug supplies.

Thus, management science may help any medical organizations to solve drug shortage crisis, it may help any organizations to attempt to reduce health care cost, one common solution for mitigating shortages is to keep more drug inventory, but drug inventory number can not be excess, in order to avoid drug out of patients (old drug) to let patients to eat in difficult. Hence, any medical organizations need to implement good pharmaceutical supply chain management strategy in order to solve drug resolve shortage challenge causes.

● How to apply management science technological tool to solve resource shortage to organization challenge?

Management science technological tool predict method may also be applied to water scarcity management aspect for government water supply organization, it may provide the scientific basis to apply optimum water resource management practices in the affected areas, methodological procedure for drought and water scarcity management or applying the economic scarcity potential method to rare earth elements highlights. It can capture resource is a useful approach as is it has an technological tool to avoid scarcity of resources to farm from atmospheric physic to robotic farm water resource shortage technological tool. A key component of this farm management approach is the use of information gathering concerns weather change. It aims to help farmers can predict when ther are enough rain supply to the farm land, they ought grow rice or fruit seed or vegetabe seed to farms. hence, it seems that management science method may be applied to help any organizations to solve natural resource or manufacture resource supply shortage challenge to any organizations.

ON conclusion, management science may be applied to resource shortage aspect, because management science is resource management technique. The two techniques are as follows: resource technique is a technique in which start and finish dates are adjusted based on resource constraints with the goal of balancing demand for resources against available supply. Any organizations may encounter resource shortage challenge. Resource scarcity is essentially about current demand for a resource exceeding available supply. Resource scarcity occurs when demand for a natural resource is greater than the available supply , leading to a decline in the stock of available resource . However, any organizational resource shortage may due to failure management, difficult management technique causes. The common types of resource management may include human resource management natural resource management, project resource management, financial management, infrastructure management , facility management enterprise asset management public asset management at organizational resource management aspects. Hence any organizations must need efficient and effective resource management strategy in order to avoid resource shortage causes.

In organizational studies, resource management is the efficient and one resource management technique choice is resource shortage solution leveling, to keep the enough stock of resources on hand, reducing both excess inventories and shortages. Any kind of resource management technique aims to ensure access to resoures and avoid supply shortages efficiency in their use, facilitate their proper and of life management, hence, effective resource management strategy may help the organization to avoid resource shortge challenge causes easily.

● Reasons to organizations need management resource strategies ?
Why ought organization implement resource managment strategies ? better

utilization means a happier and healthier team helping to reduce being overburdened and stressed. Resources are used to their maximum potential, keeping projects on time and on budget. It helps project managers keep to reduce oversights. The reasons that organizations ought to prepare effective managment science to implement the most reasonable and the most efficient and the most effective resource management strategy, because effectively managing resources can help companies more consistently deliver projects and services on time.

This is because better resource management helps to improve insights into resource availability as well as improves timelines projections. Why it is importsant to have enough resources supply and resource management strategies implementation? Resources are important for the growth to one organization, even development for any country, for example, generate energy , one need fossil fuels, and for industrial with the development, we require mineral rsources . On macro-social development aspect, natural resources are getting scarce with the increasing populatin, so it is essential to conserve them.

Why do we need resource management to organizations ? Resource management is the process of pre-planning, scheduling, and allocating the kind of resources to maximize efficiency. A resource is anything that is needed to eecute a task or project, this can be the skill set of employees or the adoption of software. Due to large organizations might be dealing with multiple projects. Effective allocation of resources help project maangers to avoid to use resources inefficiently, e.g. human resources, financial resource, physical resource and information resources. Hence, effective resource management science strategy can benefit the organization team and overall organization.

● How applying right science resource management principle to organizations

Scientific management is an attitude and a philosophy to be accepted and applied of the method of scientific investigation for the solution of the problems of industrial management . They may include experimentati, collection of data, analysis of data and formaulation of certain principles on the basic of such analysis. It aims to seek the most efficiency for plant operations. The main objective is improving economic efficiency, especially labour productivity.

However, scientific management can be summarized in four main principles to determine and standardize the one best way of doing a job . A clear division of tasks and responsibilities. High pay for high performing employee, for Toyalor's scientifi managmement principle example, he proposed that by optimizing and simplifying jobs, productivity would increase.

Nowadays, most organizations in the industry make use of scientific management, e.g. hospitals, car and computer , restaurants, among others. The advantages may include : reduction in the cost of production, better quality products, benefits of division of labour , avoidance of disputes between labour and management increased wage, gains to owners/ investors.

The main aim of scientific management is to develop all men to their greatest efficiency . The specific objectives aim to enhance production and productivity, decrease cost of production and maximize prosperity both for employer and employees having common interests (not opposite to each other).

● How Amazon e-commerce applies resource management principle to bring avoiding resource waste benefit?

For Amazon e-commerce example, it does not apply scientific management principle, due to it is not one product manaufacturing industry, it is online sale service and foreign delivery service organization. It ignores one of the key of scientific management, its creators genuinely believed that you had to pay higher wages to anyone asked to puch themselves to their physical limits. Under scientific management wages are paid to the workers as per the piece-wage system. Minimum wage is not assured, so every work needs to pay incentive wafe when he can manufacture more piece product, but Amazon believes that pay higher wages to any one can bring incentive productivity , such as it only provide online sale and foreign deli ery service to any one online buyer client, e.g. it can pay higher wage to the warehouse workers, because they need to cooperate with robotics to work hard and the human warehouse workers need to learn how to dominate any one warehouse logistic robotics to know hoe to delive and put goods to the right shelves in order to avoid to put wrong goods to the not right shelves position in warehouse.

So, in Amazon scientific management skill to workers view, its warehouse workers are smart workers, they need to know how to dominate any one warehouse robotics to do the right goods delivery to put on right shelves tasks daily. Their wages ought need to pay higher in order to avoid theig goods wrong delivery to wrong sheleves in careless. SO, Amazon feels that it needs to pay higher salary to the warehouse workers because they need have more smart and robotic control skills. When they and robotic to works together in Amazon warehouses.

So, such as Amazon warehouse workers case, Amazon ecommerce organization can apply scientific management principle to reduce resource waste. I shall explain as below:

Amazon 's warehouses have save diffent kinds of products to prepare to deliver to different countries buyers, after Amazon had confirmed that it has receive visa card payment from online channel by each online buyer successfully. So, it must have smart warehous workers, they know how to control and dominate any one warehouse robotics to cooperate to send every right shelf position message to every one warehouse robotis to know, when the warehouse robotic receives the right product delivery to the right shelf message from the warehouse warehouse, it will delvier the product to the shelf position carefully. So, avoiding none of any wrong goods putting on the wrong shelves positions occurs easily. When, every one, there has none any wrong goods are putted on wrong sheleves positions occurrence, the spending investigation time to any wrong goods putting on wrong shelves position, it does not need to any one warehouse manager to do every day, So, Amazon does not need to waste time to do any goods putting on wrong warehouse workers number, when it applies many warehouse robotics to assist them to work in order to raise goods delivery efficiency in warehouse, e.g. Amazon warehouse can apply three logistic robotics and one human warehouse worker number to do one goods shelf delivery task. Before, it needs to employ ten human warehouse, logistic workers to reponsible to do one goods shelf delivery task. I assume that the goods shelf can put total 300 pieces of different kinds of products per day. So, Amazon can reduce none warehouse logistic workers number when it increases three logistic robotics to help them to do these 300 goods delivery task per day. Hence, its wage expenditure must decrease. Moreover, logistic robotics do not feel tried , bored, overtime work, these three robotics only follow any one of warehouse worker's message to let them to know whether which kind of product is needed to put on which number of the shelf positiion. Then, these three logistic workers can remember where the product is putted on the shelf position and help any one logisitic worker to get the right product to already deliver to the foreign buyer's home from Amazon's warehouses easily, they must raise efficiency more than only workers , they work in Amazon warehouses.

Hence, Amazon believes higher wage can enourage smart logistic workers can have good performance to dominate how every logistic robot , e.g. avoiding to send wrong message to let any one logistic robotic to put wrong product to the wrong shelf number position. SO, Amazon can apply warehouse scientific management method to avoid warehouse worker individual wrong message delviery to any one logistic robotic occurrence, when they can receive higher wage, and the three logistic robotics and one warehouse worker cooperation relationship is the most suitable workers cooperation number.

Amazon 's warehouse does not need more nine workers to often move in the crowd warehouse space environment to avoid worker accident and wrong goods putting on wrong shelves number position occurrences both. Hence, Amazon can apply scientific management method on warehouse avoiding resource waste aspect, when it decides to apply logistic robotics and workers cooperation in order to avoid wasting time to investigate whether which kinds of goods are put on where the wrong shelves number positions per day tasks occurrence in possible and it can bring delay to deliver goods to the online buyer's home. it is one good example of scientific management avoiding time waste method to Amazon warehouse organization.

Can Robotic Help Warehouses To Avoid Resource Waste On Behavioral Economic View

● Behavioral economy view whether robotic can help
warehouse to avoid time and human resource
waste

IN fact,robts are being used in different types manufacturing to create more efficiency with fewer resource. Robots also reduce errors, to leass waste is produced. Less waste is produced and the robots are able to final and separate the small parts more efficiently than human hands can. For example, on environment recycled aspect, robots can help reduce waste that is incinerated by efficiently sorting materials that can be recycled quickly and more efficiently than humans reducing the input poser and cost control with such processes. So, robots can bring positive affect the environment, because robots use less energy and produce less waste.

As a whole, there are multiple benefits to using robots to fight climate change,e.g. robots can prevent pollution and emissions through careful monitoring optimize the manaufacturing processes to reduce energy consumption. Moreover, robots can help with recycling, the use of robots allows facility operators some new flexibility. Most technologies used in recycling allow to sort materials. The sensing robots (sensoes) allow robots to receive information about a certain measurement of the environment , or internal components. This is essential to robots to perform their tasks, and act upon any changes in the environment to calculate the appropriate response.

● How Amazon warehouse applies logistic robots to help
it to waste resource waste

Hence, although robots can take our jobs, because they can help organizations to avoid resource waste, and it can bring negative effect to influence we lose jobs. ON behavorioral economic view, robots can help employers to reduce employees number, but it won't influence organizational overall performance to be worse or inefficiency, such as Amazon warehouse applies logistic robots to assist workers to deliver the right kind of goods to put on every correct shelf number position rapidly every day. Hence, one logistic robot can replace at least 10 store workers to do goods delivery tasks every day, e.g. one store worker needs to spend one minute to find the right kind of good to deliver to prepare to arrange to deliver it to fly to overseas client. Logistic robots only need 10 seconds to find the right kind of goods from the near 200 number shelves in Amazon warehouse as well as they are putting 300 different kinds of goods on these 200 shelves in Amazon warehouse every day.

Because each logistic robot has very good memory. Each logistic robot must remember any kinds of goods , their putting number position on which shelf, e.g. when the worker needs to find the model laptop product from 300 different kinds of products,in Amazon warehouse. They are putting on 200 number shelves number following positions. IN general, human worker will need to spend about one minute to find the model of laptop product from these 200 number shelves in warehouse. For example, when one worker needs to find the brand Apple of one laptop product model: PHZ0123, when the warehouse has total 300 diferent kinds of products are putting on total 200 numbers of different shelves positions. Any one Amazon store worker must need to type this Apple brand laptop" Apple" name and its model number" PHZ0123 on the store computer as well as to search its putting on shelf number position from computer. Then, the Amazon store computer will find this laptop product to find its present putting on the correct shelf number position , e.g. 50 number of the shelf positon, or none stock record of all this model PHZ20123 laptop is sold out. So, Amazon store computer must need time to help this store worker to search this laptop product's putting on shelf number position as well as the worker needs time to walk to the right shelf number position to find this laptop product.

However, logistic robotic does not need to spend time to type this laptop product brand name and model number in order to search where it is putted on the shelf number position. The Amazon store worker only needs to speak this laptop product brand name, e.g. Apple and the kind of product, e.g.laptop and model number, e.g. PHZ0123 and its piece number, e.g. one piece number. Then, the Amazon logistic robot can follow the store worker's sound to find its past this kind of product's shelf number position memory to move to this shelf correct number position and finds it to deliver to the worker immediately. So, if the worker speaks 10 kinds f different products one time, then the logistic robotic can help this worker to find these 10 of different kinds products from their correct shelves numbers rapidly.

Hence, it seems that logistic robots can help Amazon store workers to reduce each product search time as well as logistic robots can help workers to do goods delviery tasks. So, in logistic robotic behevioral economic vire, logistic robotics can replace many workers to do product position research and delivery tasks, store workers only need to speak the kind of product name, model, brand name and delivery piece number to let the logistic robotic to know. Then, the logistic robotic can follow the store worke's sending message to find the product's past memmory in order to tell the store worker, whether the product has how many stocks on shelf, or none of stock on shelf and where is putted on . Hence, any one store worker does not need to spend much time to search where any kinds of products shelves number position are. They only need logistic robotics to help them to do any kinds of products deliver to , or 20 or more different kinds between products location and the store worker's location. It means that the store worker only needs to stay on the same location to wait the logistic robotic brings his products comes back after he speaks to let the logistic rotic to know whether which kinds of products and piece number he needs . Then, he checks the logistic robotic's all products where they are correct or not. He may put all of these different kinds of gatherng products to the lorry to prepare to send to airport to fly to another country to deliver to the overseas client's home immediately when he confirms that all goods are his correct. Hence, such as Amazon warehouse case, logistic robotics can help it to reduce many products searching time tasks and avoiding delivering wrong product to any overseas client's home rick occurence. Also, logistic robotics can reduce store workers number, because logistic robotics can replace 10 to 20 human store workers number absolutely. Otherwise, human store workers may have errors in their product search process, e.g. finding the wrong product from shelf or putting the product to the wrong shelf number position, but logistic robotics can reduce to 0 error to put wrong product on the shelf number position or spends long time to search the kind of product from the shelf number position. So, in logistic robotic behavioral economic view, robotics can help businesses to avoid products putting on wrong shelves number position error risk, reduce store workers number, reduce product shelf number position search economic time.

warehouse facility building resource to build any new offices, warehouses, supermarkets, shopping centers, car parks, whether they can bring global building resources reducing number to satisfy human houses living needs, if one day building resources are facing any kinds building material is reducing number, but global applying steel, wood, brick etc. different kinds of building material number increases, when global population number is still increasingm any high houses' building materials need increase, even low wood houses' wood natural resource needs increase in order to let many people can live in the expensive wood houses. SO, it brings this question: Would wood, natural resource, steel, brick resource have shortage supply challenge, due to office, warehouse, shopping center,manufacturer, ther fixed assets number building need increases, but the same time, global houses need number also increases, when polulation increases? Can businessmen their fixed assets : offices , warehouse, shopping centers, factories, supermarkets, etc. building need bring negative impact to influence future human living house resource nu mber decreases? I assume that global businessmen their offices, warehouses, shopping centers, hospitals, private school education organizations, supermarkets etc. business organizations their buildings number is sudden increasing high, due to many organizations can earn more profit to expand their businesses. So, they will need to spend much woods, steels, bricks etc. different kinds nature resources to build any high , height offices buildings in different countries. So, wood, steel brick etc. different kinds of offices building material need must also sudden be influenced to sudden increase by global business organizations increasing number. When global businesses organizations number increases, it will cause global high height offices number increases, because every business organizations must need to rent any building office to operate their businesses. If global has many new businesses are continue growing, they will influence offices building need in possibe, even for food business , e.g. supermarke, restaurant building material need will also increase, if the reestaurant can earn more profit, then it will need to expand itself restaurant vacancy floor to let many food customers do not need to spend long queue time to wait table in order to avoid to loss these food customers, even it will buy any shopping center location to build one or more than one restaurant to satisfy food customers need . So building material needs to the new restaurant design, it may decide to decorate all restaurant location, to feel food customers to feel more comfortable when they are sitting in its restaurant.SO, when the restaurant changes its inside design , it needs to find designers to buy any new building materials to design its restaurant to be new one in order to attract food customer choice.

● Green building reduces resource waste

I assume that global many old restaurants need to recorate their inside, or many global restaurants number increases, then any restaurants material natural resource need number may also be influenced to increase. Then, our earth building material resource for restaurants need will influence general office buildings material resource, shopping center building material resource decreases to supply. When, global many restaurants are needed to build, more building material resource is needed to be used build new restaurants or is needed to decorate to change old restaurants design . So, our earth will have much building material resources to be used to build new restaurants or they are be used to decorate the old restaurants design in order to change new restaurants design function. So, our earth building material natural resources for new or old restuarants , which must increase, when global has many restaurants need any kinds of building materials to be used to help them to build new or old restaurants. Then, they must influence natural resources of building material supply number to be reduced to satisfy any office building matierals user need, even any house building material user need, if global offices and houses number sudden increase. Consequently, due to global building material natural resource can not be produced rapidly in order to satisfy any office building, shopping center, house, supermarket etc. different kinds business organizations or private houses needs. Then, the natural resource of building resources shortage, it may influence any kinds of building material production price increases. It may influence global business organizations need to pay high price to rent office or build office, or build supermarket, or build shopping center, even any private houses prices increase, when global building material natural resource has no enough number to be supplied to satisfy builders' need in order to help any office, supermarket, shopping center, supermarket warehouse etc. business organization users to build their properties to operate their businesses. SO, these businessmen must need to spend much money for building expenditure, when they begin to do their businesses. Even, public or private house buyers also need to pay more expenditure to buy houses to live , when any kinds of building material price increases.

So, it explains why global business organizations number increases may influence global public or private houses prices increase, when our earth has no enough natural resource to be building matieral supplied to satisfy global construction properties development need. Finally, when global construction properties developers feel our earth building material natural resource encounters supply shortage challengem due to they need to pay higher price to buy any kinds of building material to help any business organizations to build their offices, restaurants, supermarkets, shopping centers, wareshouses etc. different fixed assets buildings or they need to ehlp any public or private houses buyers to build their houses. Consequently, any one businessmen or house livers must need to pay high price to buy any houses or offices , restaurants, hospitals etc. different buildings either to live or to use for business operations. Hence, it seems that they have chose resource supply surplus or shortage relationship between business organizations and private house buyers.

ON conclusion, I recommend that any business office buildings ought choose green buildings orrice, their advantages may include to avoid nature resource waste, improved indoor environment, quality of life , saving water, reduce , reuse, enhanced health, eco-friendly for life, reducing operational cost and maintenance , energy -efficient, non-renewable, vs renesable resource, keep it clean, protecting our ecosystem . Hence, green buildings can not only reduce or eliminate negative impacts on the environment, by using less water, energy, or natural resources.

Moreover, green buildings, or substainable design, is the practice of increasing the efficiency with wich buildings and their sites use energy , water and materials, and reducing impaction human health and the environments for lifecycle of a building. So, on environmental benefits of grren building aspect, it can enhance and protect bio-diversity and ecosystems , imprive air and water quality, reducing waste streams, conserve and restore natural resources, on economic benefits of green building aspect, it can reduce operating costs, improve occupant productiviity, enhance asset value and profits optimize life-cycle economic performance, on social bebefits of green building aspct, it can enhance occupant health and comfort, improve indoor air quality, minimize strain on local utility infrastracture, improve overall qualty of life.

Consequently, if any organizations can apply green building concept to design and build their offices, waterhouses, restaurants, shopping centers etc. different kinds of business green buildings, even ourselves houses design is chosen by green building concept. On behavioral economic view, green building concept is the best moethod to help us to reduce natural resource waste nowadays. Then, I beleive that our earth nature resources won't be easte easily.

CHAPTER SEVEN

How social resource influences organizational resource supply

Human Behavioral network job brings social economic benefits

What does human network job mean ? Why may human network job be popular? Why human network job behavior may influence economy ?
Nowadays internet is popular to use. We can apply internet to find data , search any new things, even earn money. Why does internet
may become huma network job source. For example, e-publish may be one kind of new human network job. Any authors may apply internet
channel to help them to sell electronic or paper books from e-publisher web store. They may apply facebook, you tub etc. any online
channel to promote themselves new books to let new readers to know whether when they may buy themselves favourable new topic books to read from electronic publisher web store.

Thus, future electronic publisher industry may help any authors to build internet network platform to help them to sell and promote
ot advertise their any one new electronic or paper book topic to let global any one reader to choose to buy their any new topic books from electronic publisher web store easily and conveniently. However, it implies that electronic network platform author may be one kind of future new human network job in our societies.

How electronic network platform author job may bring economy benefit in macro economy view? A person can have few friends, contacts and still

be very influential if these few
friends and contacts are themselves highly influential, e.g. one author must
not need to know any one reader in global society. When they like to choose
any electronic books from electronic internet network platform. They may
become the author's any one topic book buyer, when they feel the author's
any one topic book is fun and attract they make decision to buth the strange
author whose the topic book from electronic book publisher's platform
web store conventiently in short time. Although, they are strangers, they
do not know themselves , but the reader can understand what it way that
made Google from writing platofrm to create new creative mind and typing
network job method to replace traditional hand writing book method for
global authors. It will be one kind of new human network writing job.

Hence, global any one reader can apply an innovative search engine ,
such as google.com to find whether whom author personal new topic books
are value to read from internet.
Then, the electroniuc publisher's web store may be new book store platform
sale network to help the author to sell many electronic or paper books from
electronic network platform
in short time. So, internet may be future new network plaform to help global
any one author to create network writing job absolutely. Furthermore,
internet may be popular social media
to help any one author to build goold relationship between his/her readers.
It is one kind of new network, human network job. New authors do not need
to buy many paper books to prepare to put in any one book shop warehouse.
Their every book can print on demand to reduce out of book stock in any
one book shop. They may choose to sell either electronic books or paper
books both from any one book publisher web store. So, electronic network
platform may be one kind of good writing channel to help human authors to
create income and it can also help authors to bring new creative mind and
new topic fun content books to let readers to know and buy to read from
electronic publisher network platform.

Why does human behavior may be one kind of new human network
job to bring global economic advantages. ALthough, it may be free income
or without inocme, but the person does the network behavior, his/her
behavior may be bring advantages to influence many other people's health.
For this case, when a worker in a coffee shop in an airport gets a vaccination
againinst the flu, it does not only helps him or her stay healthy, but also helps
the many travellers who might otherwise have been inflected if that workers

caught the flu. So, the externality , the result implies the vaccination of even a part of a community conveys benefits to the whole community. For example, governments pay special attention to the vaccinations of school children, teachers, health mothers, and the elderly, categories of people particularly susceptible not only to catching, but also to transmitting a disease.

It is not accidental that governments are heavily involved with vaccination . When there are externalities, free market, fail to persuade individual incentives with society's

their the worker's decision of whether to get a vaccine ends up attracting whether other people get sick. The workers might not fully take all these other people's potential suffering into account when making her or his vaccination decision.

As Stanford University does many suggestions, understand this and tries to help them make the right decisions and so providers free flu vaccines for its staff and students.

Small pockets of unvaccinated individuals can allow a disease to gain a spread more widely well-being. For example, parent weighing the costs and benefits of a vaccine for their child is not always thinking of the consequences of that vaccination to other people. THese are markets in which subsidizing or regulating behavior can make everyone better off. Because the reason for requiring that a child be vaccinated before enrolling in school is not just to protect that child, because each child's vaccination affects others via potential contagions.

Robots take our jobs behavioral and economy influences

Robot job behavior brings economy influences

If one day robots can replace human to do simple, even complex jobs. They will bring what influences to our global societial economy.The popular economic refrain declares that the

global middle class is dying and robots will soon take our jobs, e.g. shopping center customer service jobs, library service jobs, cinema ticket sale jobs, restaurant kitchen cooker jobs,

even, bus drivers, taxi drivers etc. public transport driving jobs, accountant, doctors etc. professional jobs. Whether it is beautiful or petty matter if our future societies have many human jobs can be replaced to do from robots. Businessman must may reduce to employ employees and reduce to pay salary or wage, when robots can be replaced to do their employees tasks.

But, societies must bring unemployement rate rises , due to societies will have many people loss jobs when their employers choose to buy robots to serve their clients or do any office tasks or customer service or cleaning etc. tasks.

In micro economy view, employers may save money in long term, but in macro economy view, it will cause unemployment ratio rises , even crime rate rises when there are many people lose
jobs in societies. These models of doom, though, fail to account for the hundreds of businesses riding the waves of change in their industries when robots may be invented to replace human to do many simple , even complex tasks in our future societies.

WE may image that one small factory needs to manufacture fishes canes to sell to supermarket, the small , cheaper stuff and higher margin parts of the fishes manufacture industry. Before, this factory needs to employe many human factory workers need to help every fresh customer makeing the perfect fishing gear, designed for performance, durability, and cost in order to achieve to manufacture every fish cane in whole fished processing manufacturing stages. Every worker needs to spend about 15 to twenty minutes to finish every fish cane , till to delivery to any supermarket to sell. If this fish canes manufacturing factory can apply manufacturing robots to help them to finish any one working tasks , every robot can only spend five minutes to finish whole fresh fish cane manufacturing process. Thus, every robot can
help this factory save 10 to 15 minutes time to finsh every fish cane manufacturing process. IN fact, time is money, because when every robot can help this factory to reduce 10 to 15 minutes time to compare human worker. Then, this factory can finish about 20 fish canes in one hour if it can use robot to help it to manufacture fish canes. Otherwise, if this factory still use human workers to help it to manufacture fish canes, then it can finsh about 3 to 4 fish canes in one hour. SO, the manufacturing efficiency ensures that robots must help this fish manufacturing factory to raise fish canes number more than human workers. So, in robotic behavioral economy view, manufacturing robots must help this fish canes manufacturing factory to raise fish canes manufacturing number and deliver increasing number to supermarkets to prepare to sell every day. Robots can help this fish canes manufacturing factory bring manufacturing time saving, rising manufacturing efficiency, improving performance and reducing wages expenditure long time advantages in micro economy view. However,

manufacturing robots can also bring disadvanages to society, e.g. increasing unemployment ratio, increasing crime rate,
this factory workers will lose jobs and income, they need earn social welfare from government and increasing government finance pressure in short time, even long time in macro economic view.

Stanford University graduate program in economics, Scott lecturer explained that "in demand and supply economic theory for robots supply and demand case, robots supply number increasing may influence human workers demand number decrease. It sometimes calls " the efficient frontier".
No specific human beings were mentioned in any of economics classes. As robots supply and demand in market case, They (robots) may be purely theoretical " agents" who reached to the most reasonable sale prices in order to persuade any one businessman buyer to make manufacturing robot buying decision whether robots can help him / her to bring how much saving time , saving money, saving cost, improving performance, efficiency economic benefit before he/she plans to reduce workers number when he/ she decides to apply robots to replace human workers in his/her factory or office or any service department, e.g. cinema ticket sale service, shopping center customer service, shopping center cleaning , supermarket customer service etc. service or sale tasks. When robots can replace human to do any one of these tasks in any organizations. So, robots may be human worker agents who reached to prices the way robots would react to a software
command. There was nothing that explained why some people thrived and others did n't or why truly brilliant, hardworking people could fail when much lazier folks succeeded." Having been admitted to the Stanford University graduate program in economics, Scott lecturer hoped to get his answers there.

How robots influence our future social changing? Using the right technology can be a boon to your business in this economy. For internet example, it is easier than ever to find well-matched customers all around the world, to stay in contact with them, and to more quickly design the products they want. If you focus solely on being cutting -edge, though you risk letting the technology
take over what should be very robust relationships with your customers , employees, and colleagues. IN nowaddays society, technoligical advances and cutomation, personal
relationships in business are more crucial than ever. I mean that robots can

not replace human to serve clients to let them to feel more comfortable and passion more easily. For shoe shop case example, if the shoe shop apply one robot to serve its clients to replace human shoe salesperson to serve its shoe customers. Robots ensure that they can not persuade every shoe potential buyer to make shoe buying decision more easily when robots need to contact every shoe potential buyer. The reason is simple, because robots can not touch any one shoe buyer individual emotion very easier.

If the shoe buyer needs the robots to help him/her to choose any right shoe styles when he/she can not feel himself / herself can make the most right shoe style choice decision. The robots can not replace human shoe salesperson to make shoe style choice judgement more easily. They must need longer time to analyze whether which shoe style may be the most suitable to the shoe buyer. Otherwise, human shoe salesperson may attempt to make the most right shoe style choice decision to help any one shoe buyer to chooce the most right style shoe because he/she owns shoe style sale experience, shoe style knowledge, the most important reason is that they can feel every shoe customer individual emotion to touch whether he/she will feel comfortable or happy when they attempt to help every shoe customer to seek the most right shoe style in every shoe customer whole shoe searching processing. Othwerwise, serving robots are only one machine, they can not touch or feel every shoe customer individual emotion whether he/she feel comfortable or unhappy or happy when they need to contact them in whole shoe searching processing. Hence, I believe that some tasks robots can

not repalce human staff to do very easily. Otherwise, robots may bring disadvanatges to let any one businessman to loss his/her customers, due to robots can not touch every customer

emotion to compare human staff in service tasks more easily. Robots serving customer behaviors may cause money lose and customers number lose to the shop in micro economic view.

Intellectual human economic behaviors

What does intellectual human economic behaviors mean ? I believe that when we choose or decide to do intellectual behaviors, then our societies will be influenced to bring economic growth in consequence.I shall attempt to indicate pollution case to explain how and why eithet our intellectual or foolish behaviors may bring economic growth or recession in consequence as below:

On one hand, for air pollution social case aspect example, if we only consider to buy cars to drive for working aimr or holiday leisure aim. Then, our societies air will be polluted. Our health will be influenced to bad. Our car driving behaviors may cause global environment air pollution serously. In long tiem, global air pollution will bring our bodies health to be bad. Although, ourselves car driving behaviors may bring our driving travelling leisure enjoyment and comfortable feeling in short time, also we so not need to pay public transport fare often, but we need to compensate ourselves health economic intangible loss due to air pollution , when cars number increases, dirty air will cause ouselves health to become bad.

In the result, we will need to pay more medical expenditure when we are old age, due to ourselves bodies will become bad, due to we breathe global dirty air every day, due to ourselves cars pollute air in long time, e.g. 10 to 20 years, even 30 more without limited air pollution environment. So, driving cars behavior may be one kind of human foolish behavior and our foolish behavior may bring ourselves future long time medical expenditure absolutely.

One the other hand, water pollution social aspect, if we often keep much rubblish to pollute sea, oil exploration porcessing pollute ocean , ships gas pollute ocaen, then fishes will eat polluted food and drive dirty water, due to global ocean is polluted.

In fact, because human only to conside how to buy boats to carry on leisure enjoyment activities, or catch cruises to travel on the sea. Also, oil manufacturers only consider researching anywhere to find new oil exploration places to manufacture oil product, when their oil exploration processes pollute ocarn . Consequently, global fishes drink polluted warer or eat polluted food. They will have poison. SO, human will have high chance to eat poison polluted fishes, due to fishes are poison or are polluted. So, human is doing foolish activities, we only hope to find oil exploration places to pollute ocean or we only spend money to buy ticket to catch ships to travel anywhere in global ocean. All of these human foolish behaviors will bring pollution to global ocean. On consequently, we will need to compensate to eat polluted or dirty or poision fishes, ourselves bodies health will be bad. In long time, we need have high chance to pay medical expenditure when we are old. So, pollution case may be one good example to explain how and why human foolish behavior may influence ourselves future need to compensate serious medical loss.

All of these human foolish behavior will bring pollution to global ocean. On consequently, we will need to compensate to eat polluted or dirty or poison fished , ourselves bodies health will be bad. In long time, we will have high chance to pay medical expenditure, when we are old. So, pollution case may be one good example to explain how and why human ourselves intellectual or foolish behaviors may influence future long time economic loss or economic growth or recession in micro and micro economic view.

On another water pollution aspect hand, if we often keep rubbish to sea, oil exploration processing pollutes ocean and ships' gas pollute ocean, then fishes will eat polluted food and drink dirty water, due to fishes will eat polluted food and drink dirty sea water because the global ocean is polluted seriously.

In fact, because human only consider how to buy boats to carry on any leisure water activities, or catches cruises to travel on the sea. Also, oil manufacturers only consider any where to find oil exploratin places to manufacture oil products from ocean, when their pol exploration processes can plooute ocean. Consequently, global fishes drink polluted water or eat direty food. They will have poison. So, human will have high chance to eat poison fishes.

Otherwise, such as pollutin case, it can infuence inflation or deflation. Consequently, the reason indicates supply and demand theory. If air pollution is serious, then we will consider health issue, global cars demand number may be influenced to reduce, when global cars number demand will reduce, global car prices and supply number will need to change to fall down in order to attract or persuade global car consumers choose to make car purchase decision.

Hence, global car manufacture number and car price will be influenced to reduce, due to global air pollution issue. Consequently, deflation will occur because when the country citizen usually does not spend much extra saving money to buy car expensive goods. Money value will be low. Otherwise, if global cair pollution is not serious, human considers to buy cars to enjoy driving leisure lives. So, global car demand is influenced to increase , also global car price will also influenced to increase.

Consequently, gobal human will choose to buy cars to drive. Due to we accept to spend extra saving to buy expensive car goods. Car sale price and supply may be influenced to rise up. Money value is influenced to reduce. Inflation may be influenced, due to global car consumers number increases, we would not have extra money to spend easily. Car expensive goods expenditure influences our spending habit to avoid to make car purchase decision more easily. So, human intellectual or foolish activities may bring inflation or deflation consequency in possible indirectly in macro economic view.

On conclusion, above pollution case explain that how and why human intellectual or foolish economic behaviors may bring inflation or deflation consequency as wll as economic growth or recession consequency as well as any goods demand and supply increasing or decreasing consequency. It implies that human behavior may have indirect relationship to influence any goods demand and supply number to either increase or decrease result as well as any goods price will be influenced to increase or decrease in micro and macro economic view.

The relationship between social change and human behavior

Why does economic changes may influence human individual behavioral change? I shall attempt to indicate shopping behavior and staying at home behavior to explain their case and effect relationsip as below:

Human behavior can be influenced by economic change or economic change can be influenced by human behavior? Why does recession may influence consumers reduce shopping desire? In social recession suitation, it is possible that many people lose jobs suddenly, due to businessmen lose many customers. They need to make decision to reduce employees number in order to continue to keep businesses. Consequently, many firms (organizations) their employees may lose jobs. When they have much time, due to lose jobs, they will feel to avoid to spend too much time and money to go to shopping often. Many losing jobs people, they will often stay at homes. So, they will reduce time to go to shopping, then non essential products won't their preferable choice purchase products. Hence, recession will change many losing jobs people their shopping or consumption desires to avoid to buy non essential products often . Usually when economic boom, many people have jobs to do because consumers number must increase when many people have jobs to do. Then, many people can accept to spend money to buy non essential products often. Many people feel spend time to go to shopping can satisfy their purchase of any kinds of new products useful psychology or desire. So, recession is one good example to explain it can influence many people do not like often to leave homes to go to shopping easily. Many people like to stay at homes, becaue they feel worry about spending too much shopping time when they leave homes. Their staying home time is one good negative shopping behavior example. So, economic change may influence human individual behavior changes , they have direct cause and efect relationship in behavioral economic view.

May human behavior influence economic change? Is it possible that human behavior may bring the country social economic change in macro economic or micro behavioral economic view ? I shall indicate publishing industry example. Do you feel that if there are many students feel learning is very important when they read many books or many of students feel interesting to read or they have reading new books in habit, then it is possible that the country will have many students like to spend time to go to any book shops to choose the books, they feel that they can help they learn new knowledge. Then the country will increase students number, they often spend time to visit any one book shop every week. Their visiting book shops behavior which may become their habits. So, the country will increase students number, they often spend time to visit book shops. Also, it implies that visiting book shops behaviors may be their behavioral habits.

So, when the country has many students often spend time to visit book shops , their visiting book shops behaviors may help any one book shop to raise books sale chance. So, the country's student individual often visiting book shop behaviors, their habitual visiting book shops behaviors must may assist help any one book shop to increase books sale number absolutely.

Consequently, any one book shop , its books sale bumber must be influenced to increase to increase because the country will have many students like or feel need visit book shops habit in order to choose any suitable books to buy to read at home in order to raise themselves learning effort. When the country has many bok shops often have many students visit their book shops, then their books sale number may be influenced to increase. It explain why student individual visiting book shop behavior may help any one book shop sale number increases also.

How human productive behavior may influence economic development

May any country which citizen behavior assist themselves country development? It is one cause and effect economic question. I mean that if the country itself citicen can not concentrate mind or energy to choose to do one kind of industry in order to let themselves country can bring the most benefit, then whether the counry itself economy can bring the most serious economic benefit. I shall attempt to indicate these countries themselves indistry choice to explain whether these countries themselves citizen productive behavior may help themselves countries to achieve the largest economic benefits. I shall indicate as below:

New Zealand farmer individual wine productive behavior

For New Zealand country example, this country concerns itself effort is foucs on farming agricultural aspect. So, this country has many farmers concentrate on farming agricultural aspect. May New Zealanders choose to spend time to produce different kinds of wines, e.g. wine or red grape wine is for the people are eating meat, or they are eating dinner.

When these New Zealanders their behaviors choose to do farming or agriculture to grow and produce different kinds of taste of white or red grape wine drinking products job. Themselves grape agriculture behavior will influence these New Zealanders themselves, they can learn how to improve different kinds of grape wine drinking products in order to achieve every kinds of white or read grape wines taste improving aim during their white or red grape producing process.

Why can New Zealander every individual white or read grape wine producers improve their white or read grape wine taste more easily? In behavioral economic view, it can explain that why any one New Zealander white or read grape wine producer can be encouraged or excited or persuaded to concentrate nervous and energy and effort to learn how to improve their white or red grape wine products easily.

In fact, New Zealand is one agricultural food export country. It has good natural environment resource , e.g. land, seed to provide any one farmer to produce themselves any kinds of agricultrual food products, e.g. fruit, or wine food products. Because New Zealanders know themselves country has enough natural resource . So, in common, many New Zealanders choose to attempt to do farming agricultural jobs in order to export themselves any kinds of fruit or meat or wine products to overseas or sell to domestic in order to earn profit.

So, when these New Zealand farmers number has been increasing every year. This country farmers will feel themsleves competition between this New Zealand farmers themselves are serious due to they may feel New Zealanders choose to do agriculture businesses in order to export themselves different kinds of farming food to overseas or sell to local to earn profit.

Hence, when many New Zealand farmers feel that farmers number has been increasing every year. They will feel themselves competition is serious. They must need to spend much time and nervous and effort to research what method is the best how to produce the best taste of white or red grape wine products in order to let local or overseas wine buyers to choose to buy his/her producing white or read grpae products to drink.

Hence, in competition psychological view, may influence many New

Zealand white or reaad wine producers had been beginning to change their learning behavior on researching what method is the best in order to produce the best quality of taste red or white wine products to sell in order to attract overseas or local white or read grape wine drinkers to choose to buy his/her wine products. Their behavior will focus on learning how to raising or improving white or read grape wine taste method more than only focus on producing a large number white or red grape wine products. They believe wine quality is more important to compare wine producing number. So, New Zealand wine producers themselves wine producers behaviors have been changing on concentrating on researching wine quality method aspect more then wine producing number aspect in behavioral economic view.

America high technological productive behavior

For America example, US is one high technological country, it owns many high technological knowledge talent inventors, e.g. computer science inventors. Hence, US must attract many diferent countries owning high technological computer inventors choose to go to US to develop their computer science profession career. Also, it seems that when many computer science inventors or professions choose to go to US to develop themselves computer science new career. In behavioral economic view, due to their leaving themselves countries choice, which may bring influence themselve country job behaviors need to be changed. They must need to adapt US new live. Because they will forgive their past computer science job. These computer science professionals need to spend time to adapt US new lives. They " past computer science job behaviors" will need to be changed to their new US any computer employer's new computer science job model.

Because their traditional computer science jobs needed to be forgot in their themselves countries. They will feel their old computer science job knowledge and behavior needed to change in order to let their US any one new of computer company employer feels satisfactory to accept their new working behavior in any one US computer organization.

So, on the other hand, many US computer company employer will feel that they must need time to accept any one new overseas computer science professions their working behaviors, their working attitude daily, because these foreign comouter science professional, their past computer working behaviors and working attitude must be different to US domestic computer science professions.

In behavioral economic view, these overseas computer science professions, their working behaviors and attitude must be needed to change in order to adapt any one US new computer company itself domestic or local computer science professional stafs themselves daily working behaviors and attitude because these overseas and local computer science professionals must need to team work together.

In behavioral economic view, it is only one way that foreign computer science professionals must need to change themselves past country traditiona daily working behaviors and attitude in order to cooperate with these US local computer science professionals in teams more easily.

Consequently, if these foreign compute science professionals can change their past working behaviors and attitude to let any one US local computer science professional feels to cooperate with them easily in short time. Then, the US computer company itself whole computer professional teams themselves efficiencies will be influenced to raised or improved by the changing past working attitude and working behaviors of these foreign computer science professionals. So, in behavioral economic view, only if US any one computer company hopes itself computer teams themselves efficiency can be raised or improved when it decides to employ foreign computer science professionals and US domestic computer science professionals. They need to work in teams together. They must need to let these foreign computer science professionals to know how to change their working behaviors and attitude to let their domestic computer science professionals feel easy to work together. Then, the US computer company itself whole team efficiency must be rasied or improved easily in short time.

● China share market investing behavior

For China share market example, economic development depends on financial market. Because if many Chinese have interest to invest to carry on shares buying and selling activities in orde to learn how to earn shares interest and share profit when the China shareholder can make decision to sell himself/herself shares in the the high price, then he/she can earn money when he/she can sell the China company's shares in the high sale share price position.

If China has many Chinese like to spend time to carry on investing shares activities. Themselves shares buying and selling behaviors will influence China has many companies can increase fund from many Chinese shareholders in order to have enough money to expand or develop themselves businesses in China in long term.

Consequently, when China can have many Chinese like to attempt to carry on buying and selling shares investing behaviors in China share market. Themselves buying and selling shares behaviors can help many Chinese companies have effort to increase enough money or capital in order to continue to do their businesses in long term absolutely. So, it explains why when many Chinese become shareholders , they can assist China will have many companies continue to develop their businesses if many Chinese like to carry on shares buying and selling investing behaviors in long time in China financial investment market nowadays in behavioral economic view.

Why has any individual country have many people invest share behavior which can influence the country's macro consumption desire?

I shall apply shares market buying and selling investment behavior to explaiin why shares investment behavior which may impact the country's overal consumption desire as below:

In behavioral economic view, I assume that when the coutry has many people have interest to attempt to carry on shares buying and selling investment behavior, then their frequent shares buying and selling behaviors which may bring negactive consumption desire or shopping desire of these shares investors their consumer behavior.

The reason is simple, when the country has many share buyers number suddenly been increasing rapidly. Consequently, these large group share investors must need to spend much time to research any kinds of company shares variations, whether when their share prices will rise up of fall down in order to achieve buying the company's shares in the lowest price and selling the company's shares in the highest price level in order to earn profit.

Basic on this reason, they must need to spend much extra time to research share prices changing behavior every day, e.g. one working person will wait to leave his/her job, after he/she can spend time to gather data to research the day's share price changing behavior after dinner. So, the working person's right time may be his/her share price market research behavior. Before he/she may spend his/her night time to go to shopping after dinner, but nowadays, he/she will fogive to do his/her shopping behavior before dinner or after dinner at hight sometime. He/she will make decision to spend much night time to turn on computer to click on share market website to research his/her share purchase choice to investigate whether his/her share price whether it rises up or falls down at the moment in order to make his/her share buying or selling decision at ever night time.

I mean the when the country has many people are share investors, their shares investment behavioral spenging time which will influence many shops lose customers at might often because the country will have many people feel need to spend night time to turn on computer or watch television to investigate share price variation. So, the country will have many people / share investors choose to stay at home in order to carry on share price variation investigation behavior, they need to listen share market update news from radios or watch the share market update news from computer or TV at home every night. Consequenly, they must reduce times to leave themselves homes at night. So, their shopping behavior also will be reduced. Because these share investors feel need to spend time to investigate share price variation news at homes which can bring economic benefits (high opportunity benefits) when they choose to forgive to leave homes to go to shopping times (opportunity cost) every night.

On conclusion, it seems that when the country has many people are share investors, then their share price investigating behavior may bring negative shopping emotion at night. Consequently, the country's any one shop may lose many customers from this share investor consumer group in behavioral economic view. Hence, when the country's share investors number had been increasing rapidly, it will influence any shops lose many customers from this share investing customer group at night frequenly in short time, even long time in behavioral economic view, because their shopping desires or shopping emotion will be brought negative feeling when they make decisions to spend much time to listen radios or watch TV or computers share price update nes at night. Hence, share market will bring negative impact to influence consumer shopping desire or negative shopping emotion in behavioral economic view.

Can technology influence human shopping behavioral change?
Nowadays, technological development has reached mature stage, whether technological mature stage may bring positive or negative shopping emotion influence to global consumers. I shall aplly internet inventin or ecommerce shopping channel tool to explain whether internet technology can bring postive or negative influence to global consumer behavior in behavioral economic view.
Internet is a good technological tool, it brings e-commerce business chance. In fact, commonly, global has have many businessmen choose to use internet channel to carry on their products transactions between global

online-buyers and their electronic websites. So, global many shoppers had begun to feel online shopping is more convenient to compare visiting shops shopping. Their shopping behaviors have been changed from internet technological tool. Global has many shoppers choose to buy any products from any overseas or local businessmen their web stores. They only need to spend time to find any businessmen their webstores to choose the most suitable products to pay visa to buy from their webstores. at homes. So, in general, global had have may shoppers had changed their shopping behaviors from visiting shops to visiting webstores at homes often.

So, it seems that internet technological tool had influenced global many shops disappear, but internet webstores will be replaced their actual shops on streets. Some of businessmen either they choose webstores to replace shops or choose websotes and shops both or still keep shops only. Hence, internet tool influences global businessmen have three kinds of products sale channels to let globa local and overseas consumers to choose how to buy their products.

However, in fact, many of global shoppers, youngers and olders had begun to accept to buy any products from webstores. They feel to spend time to leave homes to visit shops , their shopping behaviors will be wasted time to not essential part to their daily lives. Hence, since internet technological invention, it had changed many consumers their traditional visiting shops shopping habit to change to buying products from webstores channel.

However, on the one hand, internet creates webstores ecommerce shopping channel to let global many consumers do not need to leave homes to go to shopping. It brings negative visiting shops shopping emotion to global general consumers nowadays. But on the other hand, it also brings positive visiting internet webstores shopping emotion to global general consumer nowadays. So, it seems that global many consumers feel that they often do not need to spend much time to go out shopping. Many global consumers feel convenient and enjoy to choose any products to buy from different internet webstores, when the online buyer chooses the most suitable product, he she only needs to pay visa card to buy the product from the online seller's webstore conveniently at home.

Hence, online shopping can bring economic benefit to online buyers, e.g. avoiding walking time or spending transport fare to visit the shop to go to shopping, shortening or reducing shopping time to do another important matter.

On conclusion, global many consumers began feel online shopping can bring more economic benefits on shortening shopping time, avoiding transport fare spending aspect. So, online shopping will be popular shopping behavior for future long time. It may encourage global many shoppers can make rapid shopping decision in short time in order to carry on any products buying transaction to global any one online shopper in short time easily in behavioral economic view. So, global many businessmen had begun to build themselves one attraction webstore in order to persuade different countries consumers to choose to click themselves webstores from internet channel to buy any kinds of products in short time easily.

So, internet technology had changed consumers traditional shopping behaviors to build positive online shopping emotion as well as raise online sellers' any products sale chance easily in behavioral economic view.

Why and how human behavior may influence the country's economic growth or recession?

When one country has many people choose to do the same matter for one period, whether their behavior may influence the country's pvera; economic growth or recession . I shall attempt to indicate cases toexplain their relationship as below:

For flowing rubblish behavioral case example, do you feel that when the country has many people often flow rubblish on the streets, instead of their flowing rubblish behavior may bring streets dirty? But, their flowing rubblish behavior may explain that this country has people may have enough money to buy food to ear, or enough cloths to wear, enough bottles of water to drink, even they may have enough money to buy new television, radio, refrigeraters , washing machines, desktops or laptops electronic home products from old to new to use in order to satisfy their living needs. So, when they flow old electronic home products, their flowing old home electronic products behaviors may seem that they have enough money to buy other new home electronic products to replace old home electronic products to use at homes.

However, it seems thaat this country ought have many people have jobs to do. So, many of them, they can easy to make purchase decison to flow any old home electronic products and buy any new home electronic products to use . Because this country has many people have jobs to do. So, they can often not use old home electonic products to become rubblishs to flow on streets after they had bought any kinds of new home electronic homes.

In fact, it also implies that this country's economy grows rapidly. So, many businesses can glow up rapdly. When they expanded their businesses, they must need to increase employees number in order to let they help themselves to raise productivity or serve their clients absolutely. So, when the country has many businesses can grow up, it seems that its economy must be better or it is improved to compare past. Due to many different kinds of home electronic products had been often bought to use by this country people in this period. So, this country's any streets can be observed that expensive electronic home products were flowed on streets anywhere. then, this country will have many electronic home products sellers can sell their home electronic products very easily. When this country has many people can find any kinds of jobs to do easily. So, due to unemploymen rate had been decreasing.

In behavioral economic view, as this many electronic home products rubblish country case, we can observe this country may have many people have jobs to do. So, consumption number has been increased long time. So, cheap food, or expensive home electronic products may be rubblish on any streets. This country's people , their flowing rubblish behaviors may be explained that many of people have enough jobs to do, so they have ability to buy any good taste food to eat or buy any kinds of expensive electronic home products to use. So, this country's economy may be improved for this long period. So, in behavioral economic view, when this country can have many electronic home products rubblishs are flowed on anywherer in streets frequently. It seems that this country will have many people have jobs to do, so it causes they often change old home electronic products or replaced them easily, when they have enough income to spend to buy any kinds of new home electronic products to use at homes easily. Moreover, their flowing old electronic home products behaviors also indicate that this country has many people their salaries may be increased in possible from their emplyers. When this country can have many different kinds of home electornic products are sold. It means that this country's electronic home products needs or demand had been increasing, due to many people have jobs to do and income increases to excite their living of needs also improve. Consequently, this country may seem have better economic improvement. We can observe from this country's electronic home products rubblish increasing income in theis period.

On conclusion, this country ought experience economic growth at this period. So, " flowing expensive electronic home rubblish increasing number " may seem that this country's economic growth is rapidly in this period, due to many people have jobs to do as well as salaries increase in this period.

Technology how impacts human behavior changing?

Technology how influences human behavior to bring changing? For example, online share purchase and sale transaction from smart phone brings share investor can do share buying or selling transation in any where and any time conveniently, non manual driving auto vehicle, bring car owner feels comfortable and spends free time to do other matter, e.g. reading, listening mucis in himself or herself car freely. electrical energy vehicle can help car owner to reduce air polluton and it can brings the drivers do not feel drive long time in any journeys in order to avoid air pollution for environmental protection responsible car drivers in our societies. Thus, they will drive long time in any journeys when they can drive electronic energy cars to replace oil energy cars.

However, online technology can also bring consumers can choose to stay at homes to buy any things from seller individual online webstore conveniently. Such as online technology can bring shoppers do not need to spend much time to visit shops to buy any things. They can choose any kinds of products from any online sellers individual online webstores conveniently at homes. Online technology excite busy consumers can make purchase decision easily as well as it can help online sellers sell any kinds of products from internet easily.

In behavioral economic view, technology can change human behavior to be improved, it can let human feels comfortable, more free time ro use, rapid making any decisions, such as apply smart phones to make share purchase or sale transaction decision, online shopping decision, even travelling any where decision in short time, when the traveller finds the most cheap hotel accommodation room price and air ticket price frm any travel agent online tourism webstore, then the potential travel customer can follow the online hotel accommodation price and air ticket price data to make decision when to buy the air ticket from the airline travel agent or make decision when to prebook which hotel accommodation room to go to the country to travel from online travel agent tourism webstores. So, technology can encourage global any country travelers to make anywhere to trvel rapidly. If the traveler can find the country's general hotel rooms and airline tickets prices had been decreasing more sightly. The traveler may make travel decision to choose the country to travel in short time, then he/she can prebook the country;s any hotel room and airline ticket to pay by visa fraom the country's any hotel and airline travel agent webstores., before one week, even one month or more easily. Hence, online technology can also encourage traveler individual frequent travel times to be increased, due to global travelers can find any hotel rooms and airline tickets prices from internet conveniently at homes. They do not need to spend time to visit any airline travel agent to enquire travel choice country's hotel rooms prices and airline ticket prices. They can compare global travel of countries choices ' all hotels rooms and airline agents air tickets prices to make prebook airline seat and hotel room decision before one week, one month even six months early.

On conclusion, online technology can encourage global travelers can make travelling any where and when traveling time desicions easily. It can excite tourism industry develops in long time. Also, such as electricity cars invention can encourage environment protection car owners do car purchase decision easily, because they can choose to drive electronic energy cars to replace oil energy cars in order to avoid air pollution occurs easily. So, electronic cars can increase electronic car purchasrs number, due to many of environmental protection attitude of car owners can choose to drive electricity cars to bring air cleans, even non -manual driving cars can encourage lazy driving and free time driving car owners to choose to buy non-manual (artificial intelligent) cars to drive , because they can spend much free time to read, listen music or do any matters in themselves cars, they do not need to drive cars, robotic (AI) auto driving machine is such one non-manual driver to help them to drive themselves cars confidently. So, non-manual driving cars can attract lazy and enjoying free time driving car owners to choose to buy to replace traditional manual cars to drive easily. Moreover, online share transaction can help any share investors to make share buying and selling decision in short time easily. When they can apply smart phones technological tool to carry on share buying and selling activities easily. They can observe any share rising or falling price suitation from smart phones in any where any any time easily. So, smart phone technology can help global any shareholders to make share purchase and sale transaction easily. So, technology can encourage human makes decision in short time rapidly.

How and why employees behaviors may influence economy development?

In behavioral economy view,I believe the country's any organizational employees behavior may bring indirect relationship to influence the country's long term economic development. I shall indicate past manufacture industry social development period to explain their relationship. For many countries' past business activities had belonged to manufacturing industry, such as US, UK past before 1980 year, it focused on steel manufacturing and steel manufacturing related machine products. So, US, Uk developed countries manufacturing industries may be past main country's economic income sources. I assume US , UK past had one million number different kinds of industries. They ought had about seven houndred thousand number organizational businesses were belonged to manufactured industry. They may include:

Steel manufacturing and steel related machine manufacturing, e.g. vehicle manufacturing, home appliances, e.g. washing machine, television, radio, refrigerate cooler, heater, air condition etc. different kinds of different kinds of steel -related manufacturing machine, they were manufactured from US, UK steel machine manufacturers. So, US, Uk the other three hundred thousand number industry may be general service industry, e.g. hotel service, restaurent, cinema, public transport service, tourism lesiure , wine bar, supermarket etc. different kinds of non-manufacturing industries business organizations were operated in UK, US past before 1980 year.

So, in UK, US developed countries industry development history, they ought have high percentage of businesses belonged to steel related manufacturing machine and steel products. Also, in the past before 1980 year, US, Uk business employers , they employed many workers are manufacturing workers. They needed to spend long time to work in factories. They were skillful workers, and they are trained to manufacturing cars, washing machine, television, heater, etc. even steel itself different kinds of steel related products to prepare to deliver to their shops to sell to US, Uk local or overseas clients.

So, I believe that past UK, US ought employ many employees, they belonged to skillful manufacturing workers, manufacture increasing steel machine or steel related machine number of products rapidly daily. So, if UK, US had had many of these manufacturing factories owned high skillful workers, then their manufacturing steel-related machine or steel both kinds of products number must be influenced to raise rapidly. Consequently, their steel machine manufacturing products would been exported to overseas or would been sold to local both markets , they may be influenced to raise sale number. They (these manufacturing workers) needed to be trained to know how to manufactur these different kinds of machine products in the efficient teams and they ought to be trained to raise their efficiencies in order to shorten time to manufacturing many kinds of steel related manufacturing machine or steel itself products rapidly. So , if their efficiencies and manufacturing performance was improved, these US, UK any one manufacturing worker and their teams ought achieve raising productivities significantly.

Hence, when past UK, US manufacturing industry development period, if these two countries' any manufacturing factories could have many manufacturing workers could be trained to be skillful and proficient manufacturing workers. Then, in past every day to these factories workers, they ought help their steel or steel related manufacturing employers to raise any kinds of machine or steel products number in every team. So, when past in the manufacturing industry development, US, UK could have many factories' manufacturing workers themselves steel or steel related machine products manufacturing skill could be trained to to improve to any kinds of these machine or steel manufacuring products quality as well as their products number could be influenced to raise by themselves skillful improvement significantly every day.

Then, what would be influenced to occur to past UK, US manufacturing industry period? In behavioral economic view, when these two manufacturing industry developed countries, such as UK, US , if they had many factories workers can be trained to improve their skill in order to achieve any kinds of steel or steel-related machine products quality could be improved as well as products manufacturing number could be also increased absolutely.

In consequence, past UK and US both countries ought increase themselves any kinds of steel and steel related machine products number to be supplied to themselves local shops to let local clients to choose any one kind of machine manufacturing products to buy easily as well as they could also export to supply overseas any countries to buy their different kinds of steel or steel related machine products to let overseas steel or steel related manufacturing machine product buyers, they can have many of these different kinds of these steel or steel-related different kinds of manufacturing machine from UK and UK these both countries easily to compare other countries.

On conclusion, I believe that past US, and UK macro manufacturing industry income GDP would increase significantly. So, they would have good economic growth performance because when many of these manufacturing workers themselves manufacturing effort could be improved. So, it explained when employees manufacturing abilities can influence economic growth indirectly.

Robots invention whether they can help organizations to raise efficiencies or inefficiencies?

In behavioral economic view, in any organizations, when the organization hopes its worker teams can raise efficiencies , the organization may choose to increase more workers number and/or it can provide training to improve these workets themselves skills in order to raise their efficiencies. For one warehouse example, when the warehouse increases many goods , they are needed to delivered these goods from the shelves to the delivering destination locations. If this warehouse supervisors feel these workers themselves goods delivery speeds are slow, which is possible due to this warehouse's workers number is not enough. So, this warehouse supervisor ought increase workers number in order to increase their goods delivery speed in order to deliver goods from the shelves to every indicated goods delivery destination in order to let any one lorry driver can transport the right kinds of goods and ensure the accurate goods number to transport to any one client home rapidly.

However, if this warehouse supervisor planed to buy several warehouse goods delivery robots to assist these warehouse workers to find the right kinds of goods from shelves and then deliver to the right destination location in the warehouse. So, these warehouse orkers can concentrate on counting the accurate goods number and ensuring the right kinds of goods in order to prepare to let lorry drivers to transport these goods to these goods of buyers themselvers homes rapidly. Consequently, in the first step, robots can concentrate on finding th right goods from shelves and delivers them to the right goods transportation of location destination. Then, in the second step, these warehouse workers can concentrate on counting the accurate goods number and ensuring the right kinds of goods in order to prepare to put them to the lorry. Consequently, when warehouse robots and warehouse workers can cooperate to work together, the most important, robots, can deal on finding the right kinds of goods and deal on delivering the accurate number of goods of job duty as well as these warehouse workers can only concentrte on counting the right kinds of goods number in order to avoid it has none any mistake of wrong kinds of goods and inaccurate goods of delivery number to be transported to the lorry and to deliver to any one buyer's home.

So, it seems that warehouse robots ought help any one warehouse worker to raise himself efficiency and avoid goods delivery of mistake occurrence easily as well as their help to warehouse workers that can let any one goods buyer feels their goods can be delivered to their homes rapidly. Moreover, warehouse robots can also help these warehouse workers to raise efficiencies because warehouse robots can help them to shorten goods delivery time between any one shelf and any one goods delivery destination of location in the warehuse because robots may help them to find the right kinds of goods from the right shelf in the short time. So, any one worker does not need to spend long time to seek anywhere is the right shelf location for the kind of goods when the kind of goods are needed to deliver to the buyer's home from lorry. Warehouse robots can help them to do this aspect of " finding the goods from the right shelf in short time job duty". So, any one warehouse worker only needed tospend less time to do the counting of any right kind of goods number and ensuring the right kind of goods job duty. Consequently, this warehouse 's any one worker, his any one kind of goods delivery time may be reduced, because robots' assistance and they may have more confidence to avoid mistake to deliver the wrong number of goods and/or the wrong kind of goods to any one goods buyer's home.

On conclusion, it seems that warehouse robots ought may help any one warehouse worker to raise efficiency for any one team in the warehouse as well as the warehouse any one supervisor does not need to spend much time to observe any one worker individual performance for " goods delivery job duty aspect" because their goods delivery job duty that had been replaced to do by these several warehouse robots. Robots can achieve the more accurate of right kinds of goods and the right number of goods delviery job performance to compare any one of human warehouse worker themselves right kinds of goods of delivery and right number of goods of delivery job performance. So, when robots can participate to cooperate with this warehouse's any one worker to do their goods of delivery job duty in this warehouse every day. Then, robots can raies any one of supervisor individual confidence in order to let they do not need to spend time to observe any one of worker individual whose goods of delivery job performane. They can concentrate on supervising any one worker whose goods transport to lorry in the final step in order to avoid to deliver wrong goods number and / or wrong kind of goods to any one goods buyer's home every day. Consequently, this warehouse's overall teams of their delviery of goods performance many be improved by robotss' participatin to goods of delivery task as well as this warehouse's oveall teams themselves efficiencies may be influenced to raise by robots' goods of delivery task participation.